BRIDGE: BIDDING NATURALLY

322-2
4

BRIDGE:

BIDDING NATURALLY

Joe Amsbury

Foreword by
Omar Sharif

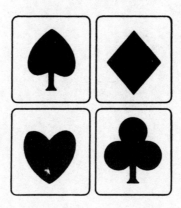

Batsford Bridge Series Editors:
Tony Sowter and Joe Amsbury

B T BATSFORD LTD London

For Robert and Julia

First published 1979
© Joe Amsbury 1979

ISBN 0 7134 1619 X

Printed in Great Britain by
Billings Ltd,
London, Guildford & Worcester
for the publishers
B T Batsford Ltd,
4 Fitzhardinge Street, London W1H 0AH

Contents

Foreword
by Omar Sharif

Every bridge player will know of my love for the game and many will know that I am particularly interested in the bidding. I was once asked in an interview if we were reaching the ultimate in bidding. I replied that I could see no end to bidding development. If there was, bridge would not be the great game that it is. The marvellous thing is that it is like looking into a telescope and being in awe of the endless sky — but — you build a bigger telescope and find that you were looking only at the fringe. You will never know the thirteen cards your partner holds, but we can keep seeking ways to get closer to finding out.

I like artificial systems, but I do not like 'one way' artificial methods where one player always takes control. I want also to exercise my judgment and to be able to bid *with* my partner. In my view the traditional natural methods are outdated. You have to be very good to achieve international results with obsolete weapons and even those who are very good have trouble. In the past card play was very important, but nowadays, with a few exceptions, there is not so very much difference in top card play standards. Players have learned so much and they know how to pass accurate information in defence. Of course you are at a big disadvantage if you are often called upon to exercise your judgement, rather than have a whole armoury of bids at your disposal.

A natural basis for bidding can only be good enough if it includes a comprehensive selection of treatments and understandings. The Sharples brothers in England do not play what I call Acol any more than the top American players play Goren or Standard American. Many world class players play what they call natural bidding but it is in fact a highly ornate and conventional machine. There are many, many areas of bidding that have not been fully analysed and discussed, many idle bids not put to good use. If we call bidding a conversation then English is as good a language to speak as any other. However, to obtain anything like the maximum degree of communication, you must have a complete understanding of the structure and a very wide vocabulary. Some players have done an enormous amount of study and analysis in order to give their natural methods this wide vocabulary. It is good that the results of some of this industry have been produced in a book that is easy to read, and as someone who has been constantly involved in this non-stop evolution, no one is better qualified to do the job than this author.

Omar Sharif

Introduction

If you are a beginner, this book is not for you, unless you are prepared to do some work. But if you have achieved a certain standard as a natural bidder, and believe that your bidding is sound, please read on. Why? Because I think you will find that as far as bidding is concerned you are still very much a beginner.

First let us define natural bidding. It means simply that clubs mean clubs, that if you sound strong you are, and that you try to describe your hand to your partner in a natural recognisable fashion. Of course there must be some artificiality, from simple Stayman to a plethora of conventional aids. But the roots of natural bidding are deeply founded in common sense logic.

I have carefully avoided using the word Acol. Most of you would claim to play Acol, or Goren or Standard American, but it is certain that if you meet ten Acol pairs in a row, you will also meet ten different systems. Unless you are in the top class it is probable that your methods are a tangle of half-memorised and badly analysed muddle.

The more hard working of you no doubt try to plug the holes in your constantly leaking vessel, but always leave a hole somewhere else. Yet you probably think that you bid well enough, and that it is the system that is inefficient.

It rarely occurs to players that bidding, whatever the system, is simply an exchange of information. A system is a language. For the sake of the argument let's assume that 'natural' bidding is English, and other systems are the native tongues of Italy, France or Spain. Good bidding is akin to an erudite conversation, and for this it is not enough to learn just the three letter words; you need the whole vocabulary. It is as foolish to say that Precision Club is a better system than Acol, as it is to say that Italian is a better language than English.

It you accept that bidding is a conversation, it becomes obvious that for partners to communicate well they must speak the same language. It also follows that the greater the mastery of the language, the greater the degree of definition and understanding. Masters of a language can say similar things in a variety of ways, adding depth by way of emphasis and subtle nuance, so that there is no possible misinterpretation of meaning.

Great writers and poets convey meaning with a rich clarity that makes us wonder why we did not think of it before. Great bidders achieve some of the same lyricism and harmonious discourse, whatever the vehicle that we call 'system'. All the best bidding partnerships have a rhythm that comes from a good language, with a large vocabulary, and a depth of definition and a well-integrated structure that has been built by hard work.

All that aspiring pairs have to ask themselves is, what is the method best suited to them, or even, what is the best method? It is logical that they will be influenced by success, and thus the methods of the great Italians spring readily to mind. Many pairs turned in their dismay at their own inefficiency to Blue Club or Precision Club, were very pleased with their obvious improvement, and blessed their new found language.

But they overlook the fact that it is probably the first time in their bridge lives that the two partners have really got together to learn and discuss a comprehensive system. In fact when the Italians were winning their many world championships, they were spearheaded by players using the Roman and Neapolitan Club systems. The great Blue Team did not transfer allegiance to different methods and find that overnight they were as fluent as ever. They transferred to another soundly based vehicle, and then went about the task of really learning the new language.

The great advantage of a naturally based system is the lack of strain on memory. Its greatest weakness is an apparent lack of need for study. It is so easy to assume that Acol, for instance, is easily learned; because a few lessons and a little discussion can readily be assumed to be sufficient. In fact even a natural system takes a lot of time and effort to learn, and just as it may take a long time to become fluent in a new language, so it takes time to assimilate the vocabulary and articulation that is available even in a natural system.

Without getting into pointless argument about the relative merits of different methods, and bearing in mind that we are talking of just one aspect of the game, bidding, the difference in the ultimate efficiency of the various main systems is arguably minimal. There is nothing archaic about a natural exchange of information, nothing lacking in its potential. The mighty Italians were eventually unseated by a team using natural systems, albeit very complete and definitive natural systems.

Players like Bob and Jim Sharples, Jack Marx of England, Murray and Kehela of Canada, Kantar, Kaplan and Sheinwold of America, have put an enormous amount of work into giving natural bidding great depth. This evolution is a never ending process, for the roots are strong and lend themselves readily to adjustment and addition without becoming unwieldy. There is a flexibility that a computerised system will never attain, and a facility for shrugging off the attempts of the enemy to gum up the works. It is impossible to give due credit to all the countless players who have added to the repertoire, but in general I have pinched the basic structure from the Sharples/Marx formula that has not only proved as good a bidding method at the table as any other I have seen, but has also kept pace with the new thought that comes from all directions in this increasingly competitive game.

So to all players who are so far loyal to a natural base, I would say that it is undeniable that if you reach the right spot with high frequency you will be very difficult to beat. I hope this book will prove that you can reach this desired efficiency with the system you have been using. It is not so difficult to learn, but much more difficult to convince you that you have not yet begun.

By way of acknowledgment, I would like to say a special thank you to my next door neighbour Mick Foster, for the many laborious hours he has spent typing out my manuscript and to Lawrence Young for the countless hours spent on improving my English.

Chapter 1.
Opening Bids

It might be thought that in a book designed for the average or better player who aspires to top class, little need be said about an opening bid of one. This is not the case. We can leave for a moment the opening bid of 1NT which needs separate discussion. The world is heavily populated with average bridge players and a good many of them remain average for one simple reason; they have forgotten what it is like to be a beginner.

When you begin to learn the game, certain basic principles have to be explained, but the importance of these principles does not always register. However, the basic principles behind the concept of the opening bid are unaltered, no matter how strong a player may become.

The opening bid is the beginning of a conversation between two partners who hope to discuss and arrive by mutual agreement at the best final contract. If communications are to be lucid, there are certain basic principles to remember. The first is that if opener begins with one of a suit, and his partner makes an unlimited response, i.e. a bid of another suit, then opener guarantees to bid again. Without this promise there can be no sensible or lucid conversation.

However, opener must consider how best to fulfil this promise, and at the same time give a more complete and accurate description of his pattern and strength. Many players learn by rote to open the higher of touching suits, and the lower of non-touching suits. Then as they develop they find that there are certain exceptions to these rules. But, in adopting the exceptions, they tend to overlook the basic principles behind how a choice, if it exists, should be made.

There is obviously no problem when opener has only one suit to bid. But when there are two or more possible alternatives, care must be exercised in choosing which bid to make first. Beginners learn that, with four hearts, four spades and three — two in the minors, there is a danger of missing a heart fit if opener bids 1♠ and partner responds 1NT. With an opening bid of 1♥, however, there is less danger that a spade fit will be missed.

So far so good, but this principle has been prostituted to the extent that players always open 1♥ with four spades and four hearts, without any consideration of the possible outcome. Players go so far as to say that if they open 1♠ and rebid 2♥ they guarantee at least five spades and four hearts. While there will be a higher frequency of hands when the first bid suit is longer than the second, this should not be considered an inflexible rule.

Nowadays, most natural bidders would chose to open 1♥ holding the following hand:

♠ A K x x   ♥ A K x x   ♦ Q x x   ♣ x x

for the reasons previously stated. Should partner respond 2♦, they would rebid 2NT, which undoubtedly shows the hand type and strength fairly accurately. However, they forget the danger of suggesting no-trumps as a final resting spot with no guard in clubs, and the possibility that should no-trumps be the best final strain, the hand might best be played from the other hand.

Of course, if you open 1♠ and partner responds 1NT there is danger that you might lose the heart suit but, under normal circumstances, 1NT will not prove to be a silly contract, and all bidding should be designed to avoid silly contracts while still trying to find the best one. If there must be an area where there is a loss of efficiency then logic suggests that there is less to lose in being slightly wrong in a low level contract, than in being wrong at the game level or higher.

This idea of the amount of gain or loss is not given the importance that it deserves. Very often a balanced hand, which usually causes the trouble, can be dealt with by opening 1NT; but should the hand not be within the prescribed range then an alternative bid must be found. As discussed later, one of the best reasons for supporting the use of a weak no-trump is that it solves most of the bidding problems of weak balanced minimum opening bids, which cause the most trouble when playing a strong no-trump. Many good players do use a strong no-trump but, by and large, they overcome its pitfalls by employing the judgement that has come from years of top class experience.

With, for instance:

♠ A J x x   ♥ K Q x x   ♦ Q J x   ♣ x x

most players would agree that the hand should be opened. There is no problem playing a weak NT, but with a strong NT, an alternative must be found. All the problems mentioned earlier now exist. With an opening bid of 1♠, a heart fit is missed when partner responds 1NT. If he responds 2♣/♦, opener can hardly rebid 2NT, because that is mathematically unsound; and he cannot rebid 2♥ if this is supposed to guarantee at least five spades.

There is a way round this dilemma. With 4—4 in the majors and a balanced minimum hand, opener should first bid his three card minor suit. With a three card club suit, there is never any serious bidding problem. After 1♣ —1♦, opener rebids 1♥. From responder's point of view, opener would bid the same way with a 4—4—1—4 shape; and so with the values to proceed, responder should always next bid 1♠ with a four card spade suit so as to ensure that a 4—4 spade fit is not missed.

Should the three card suit be diamonds, there is no problem if the bidding starts 1♦ —1♥/♠, since opener can simply support. When partner responds 2♣, the problem can be circumvented by agreeing that a rebid of 2NT shows a hand that is minimum and balanced. I can almost hear you asking 'What happens if partner raises the minor suit?'. Well, we all learn in the cradle not to support a minor suit when there is any attractive alternative available, and should the bidding go 1♣ —2♣ or 1♦—2♦ you can pass, if not happily, then with a certain amount of contentment. It will often be the best contract, and it will never be a ridiculous one.

Another age old problem occurs when opener is 5—4 in touching suits, and the shorter suit is higher ranking. The whole structure of natural bidding has been influenced by the 'Baron' theory, that opener should always begin with the higher of touching suits, whether or not the higher suit is one card shorter than the lower.

This theory almost went as far as to propose that with:

♠ 5 4 3 2   ♥ A K Q J 10   ♦ K x   ♣ x x

the correct opening bid should be 1♠. Following this reasoning through, it was argued that by bidding 1♥ opener denied a spade suit unless he had the strength to make a reverse and show both suits in natural style. It would strike most players as nonsense to open this hand 1♠.

However, experience shows that to adopt as a general principal, the style of bidding first the higher of two touching suits rarely leads to serious problems, and often leads to considerable gain. Even the most reactionary of natural bidders would open 1♠ and rebid 2♥ when holding:

♠ A K J x   ♥ Q 9 x x x   ♦ K x   ♣ x x

If responder then gives preference to spades with something less than ideal support, at least the suit is robust enough to provide a playable spot.

If opener insists on starting with a bid of 1♥, his five card suit, and his partner bids two of a minor, he will have to bid again. The only bid available with his minimum values is a rebid of his moth-eaten heart suit. But if he opens 1♠ he can then rebid 2♥, at least showing both suits.

Some players get hag-ridden with worry about being given false preference and having to play with an insecure trump holding. But it is no more than common sense that by offering two alternative trump suits a hand must, on balance, be more accurately bid than by mentioning twice only one poor suit. Each player must decide whether or not to stick to the archaic idea that the longest suit must always be bid first irrespective of the relative strength of the two suits. It you do, then you will no doubt join the growing ranks of players who claim natural bidding is inefficient.

Most bidders would open 1♦ with the following hand:

♠ x x x   ♥ x   ♦ A K J 9   ♣ K Q x x x

It is obviously preferable to open 1♦ and rebid 2♣, than to open 1♣ and rebid 2♣ after a major suit response. There is no theoretical disadvantage. But change the hand slightly to:

$$\spadesuit \text{ x} \qquad \heartsuit \text{ x x x} \qquad \diamondsuit \text{ A K J 9} \qquad \clubsuit \text{ K Q x x x}$$

Do you still open 1♦? Bearing in mind that the whole object is to get to the right contract, or at least to a sensible contract with the maximum frequency, it could now be dangerous to open 1♦.

In the first example, if the bidding proceeded 1♦–1♠/2♣–2♥, we would have been well placed to give preference to spades and feel that the job has been well done. In the second case, if the bidding proceeded similarly 1♦–1♠–2♣–2♦–2♥, we would have quite a problem. 2♥ can only be construed as a forward going bid, and does not promise a heart suit. This is not the time to go into the 'fourth suit forcing' theory, but suffice to say that one is not allowed to pass.

What you now choose to do with the hand is your problem. The point is that if responder is two suited in the majors, after an opening bid of 1♦ there is no way that the hand can be played in hearts at a low level, and in many cases no way that the hand can be played in hearts at all. But with an opening bid of 1♣, the bidding would proceed 1♣–1♠/2♣–2♥. This would now be a natural bid, and opener could make a more or less contented pass.

In choosing his first bid, opener is governed by the need to look ahead, and by the basic promise he has made that after an unlimited response he will make a second bid in order to keep the bidding open.

Another hand that readily justifies the logic of good bidding, but is consistently misbid, is a hand with 4–3–5–1 distribution. Holding, for example:

$$\spadesuit \text{ K Q x x} \qquad \heartsuit \text{ A x x} \qquad \diamondsuit \text{ K 10 x x x} \qquad \clubsuit \text{ x}$$

most players would open 1♦. There are enough occasions when partner responds in a major, making life comfortable, for players to overlook what happens when partner responds 2♣. I think Norman Squire has summed it up very well when, in a slightly different context, he commented that if the bidding should go 1♦–2♣–2♦ and you arrive in a grotesque contract facing a singleton, it is all too easy to say, 'That was unlucky'. It was not unlucky.

In fact you have just been lucky on those occasions when partner made a convenient response in a major. Of course, you should open 1♠. Now there is no rebid problem, over 1NT or 2♣, you can support hearts, and no-one should have any trouble in dealing with a response of 2♦.

Make the spades weaker and the diamonds stronger and then, very probably, I will have lost a number of converts. Of course, it is now much less likely that a low level diamond contract will be completely bad, but it does not alter the principle that it must be right to show two suits with a minimum opening hand, rather than just one, if sensible contracts are to be reached with the maximum frequency.

Responder, with 9 or 10 points, might have six clubs and four of the major. One can then imagine some people playing these hands in 2♦, and going down, with 4♠ in the ice box.

4—4—4—1 hands ceased to be a problem when the early theorists suggested starting with the suit below the singleton. But nowadays we know that with:

♠ K J x x   ♥ K Q x x   ♦ K J x x   ♣ x

it is best to open 1♥. This is because an opening bid of 1♥ will guarantee that we miss neither a heart nor spade fit, and should partner respond 1NT or 2♣ we can rebid 2♦. This is not so comfortable for those who insist dogmatically that when they bid two suits, they guarantee at least five cards in the first.

The passage of time seems to erode basic principles, as players exhibit their inventive flair and create new innovations. Without this constant evolution there would be no progress, but in bridge, as in many other fields, there are in fact certain principles that will never change.

We will not go far wrong if we keep in mind the basic idea that an opening bid of one of a suit says 'I have at least four cards in this suit and would like to suggest it as trumps'. If we then bid a second suit, we promise that we have at least four cards in this suit also, thus showing partner two potential trump suits.

With two touching suits we usually open the higher first. It then follows quite naturally that if we open 1♥ and then rebid spades, we have at least one more card in hearts than in spades. We also show considerably more than minimum values by bidding our longest suit first and then 'reversing' into our second suit. There has been no consideration of economy with this sequence, since if responder wishes to give simple preference with a minimum he must raise the contract to the three level. Thus, logic suggests that if we bid two suits in this natural but uneconomic fashion, we must have sufficient strength to feel that our combined values will provide a playable spot at the nine trick level.

What would you open with:

    ♠ A Q 7   ♥ K Q 6   ♦ A 9 8 7   ♣ A 10 8 ?

If, as most, you choose the automatic 1♦, you will most likely get a convenient response and arrive in the best contract. But if partner responds 2♣, and you rebid 3NT (what else?) he will have to guess right as to whether or not to press on, as you could have anything from a good 16 to a bad 20 points. Open 1♣ and then you are sure to be able to jump to 3NT to show 19 balanced points. The philosophy is important. If you have no immediate rebid problems, be careful to choose an opening bid that avoids future problems.

Chapter 2.
Bidding No-Trumps

The first thing that partnerships agree is the strength of an opening bid of 1NT. There would appear to be no general reason why one particular range should be chosen rather than another. There is, however, a practical advantage in confining the range to a difference of only 3 points, so that the subsequent definition of the hand becomes much easier.

Many partnerships vary the strength of the opening 1NT with the vulnerability, and with the new fashioned Mini No-Trump (10–12 pts) it even depends on the position at the table. So a partnership may vary the strength of its NT opening bids into as many as three different ranges. To me the Mini No-Trump just creates fun for those who use it, and seems akin to shooting arrows into the air and then wondering where they will eventually come down.

Many partnerships opt to use a weak no-trump when non-vulnerable, and a strong no-trump when vulnerable. But it does not seem sensible that an opening bid which is based on sound premise becomes less efficient when the vulnerability changes. Also it seems that few players recognise that when they change the strength of their 1NT bid, many of their constructive auctions are also changed, and in fact they end up playing two different systems. This is not desirable in terms of memory, nor efficient in terms of the development of method or the rhythm that is built up from long practice.

Of course there is the obvious risk of giving a big penalty by opening a relatively weak hand 1NT when vulnerable. But there is the parallel risk with the strong no-trump of reaching the wrong contract from lack of definition. Not too long ago I had the pleasant experience of playing against a good pair who were playing a strong no-trump vulnerable, when the following hand occurred:

♠ 8 6 2
♥ K 5 3
♦ Q 4 2
♣ K J 7 2

Opener dealt and bid 1♣, I overcalled 1♠, this hand as responder then bid 2♣ and my partner 2♠. This was passed back to responder who chose, not unreasonably, to persist with 3♣. This was doubled and went down 800. Opener had:

♠ 9 7 3
♥ A Q J 4
♦ A 6 5
♣ Q 6 5

and his choice of 1♣ was forced on him by his system, since he could hardly open 1♥ and risk a response of 2♣ or 2♦, to which there would be no comfortable rebid, except for an unsound 2NT or a raise of responder's minor with the risk of playing at too high a level with an insecure trump suit.

A few hands later the bidding went 1♣—1♥—2♣—2♥/Pass— Pass— and back to the West hand shown here. The decision was to pass, and 2♥ was duly made with East/West holding:

♠ 5 3 2		♠ A 8 4
♥ 10 7		♥ 8 6 5
♦ A Q 6 2		♦ K 9 5
♣ Q 10 8 7		♣ A K 6 5

It can be seen that 4♣ is a fairly comfortable contract.

The remonstrations fell on deaf ears, as there was no valid answer to the argument that a short while before, a very similar hand had led to a heavy penalty. Their bidding seemed all very safe, but the 'safety' had led to a loss of 16 IMPs. It is pointless arguing that they had bid badly of the strong no trump; it was just their system. Those who play a weak no trump would have had no problems since clubs are clubs.

It is obviously easy to produce hands to bolster a particular argument, and we want to talk of good theory and sound practice. Most Precision Club players use a 1NT opening bid that, being 13—15 points, can hardly be regarded as strong, and no-one claims that the method is unsound or even dangerous. I fail to see how a natural method that employs a 12—14 point no-trump becomes that much more perilous for the sake of a single point.

Most players like to hear partner open 1NT, unless like me they occasionally have a personal objection to him playing the hand. In one bid the hand is narrowly defined both as to type and strength. It follows naturally that the more frequently the bidding starts with 1NT, the less often there will be bidding problems. Allied to an integrated and definitive transfer method, almost any responding hand can be bid with a high degree of accuracy after a 1NT opening. A suggested transfer method is included in the chapter on conventions.

Another advantage of always using a weak no-trump is parallel to Sherlock Holmes's dog that did not bark. At the table, whenever partner makes an opening bid other than 1NT, I am much better placed in a competitive auction in knowing that partner is not balanced with 12—14 points; he must either be too shapely or too strong to open 1NT.

It also follows that, when using a weak no-trump, an opening bid of one of a major shows a five card suit with considerable frequency. A little analysis will show that a balanced hand with 15 points and a major suit, especially spades, of only four cards, would nearly always open with a bid of some lower ranking suit. Thus, in competition it is quite safe to raise an opening bid of one of a major with three card support, and on occasions this can solve such high-level bidding problems as the following:

North	East	South	West
1♠	2♥	3♣	3♦
Pass	Pass	?	

South holds:

♠ 8 4 2   ♥ K 4 2   ♦ J 5   ♣ A K 8 5 2

North was going to rebid something. It now appears that it wasn't diamonds, hearts or no trumps; so he must have rebiddable spades.

In regular partnerships I believe that an opening bid of 1NT should still be made on a balanced hand, even when it contains a five card major suit. Obviously it does not make sense to open 1NT with a hand such as this:

♠ 6 4   ♥ A K J 10 8   ♦ A J 4   ♣ 6 3 2

You should open and rebid the strong heart suit.

But consider another possibility:

♠ Q 8 7 4 2   ♥ K 6   ♦ A 10 4   ♣ K J 3

If you now open 1♠ and partner makes a natural unlimited response, you have to rebid your moth-eaten spade suit. In fact you can choose to describe this minimum opening bid, either by saying that you have a balanced hand with about 13 points, or by saying that you have about 13 points based on a spade suit. There can be no doubt which is the more accurate description.

If after first bidding a suit, opener rebids no-trumps, it is logical that this should show a hand above the range of a 1NT opening bid. My own view is that, especially when using a type of Crowhurst machinery, a 1NT rebid should carry a little more range than the usual norm of about 15—16 points. We use a range of 15—17 points, and the Crowhurst 2♣ convention can then be employed by responder to gain more precise information about the hand structure and strength. We shall come back to this later.

Now a jump rebid in no-trumps by opener, such as 1♦—1♥—2NT, can cover a range of 17—19 points. Yes, I know that I have suggested rebidding 1NT with 17 points and also rebidding 2NT with 17 points, but we all know the tremendous difference in trick potential between one 17 point hand and another. It is for you to decide which category to place your 17 points, but from responder's point of view the 2NT rebid will be assumed to be about 18 points.

There is a murky area when opener receives a response at the two level. The sequence 1♥—2♣—3NT, can show anything from a well fitting 16 points such as the following:

♠ A 10 9   ♥ A J 10 7 2   ♦ A 9   ♣ Q J 9

up to and including a bad 20 points; and this is an almost untenable range. For this reason, many partnerships now agree that after a two level response, 2NT should be regarded as forcing. This has much to be said for it, since the worst that can happen is that you will reach the occasional game on slightly insecure values. This is not a bad fault since aggression is the key-note of the modern game.

However, if the 2NT rebid shows 15 to a bad 17 points, responder can always opt to pass with an unsuitable minimum. The advantage comes with the jump to 3NT, i.e. 1♥—2♣—3NT, which allows responder to assume that opener has 18—19 points, and he is then very much better placed in deciding whether or not to proceed towards a slam.

The sequence 1♥—2♣ then 2/3NT—5♣ is just about unheard of. A point I have often made in discussing bidding is that solid suits tend to be very much undervalued. Nothing much can go wrong with a solid suit and I would, therefore, recommend that this sequence should show a solid suit with about 7/8 tricks. It may be a solid six card suit plus another trick or a solid seven card suit with nothing outside. The following hand from match play illustrates the point:

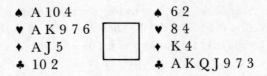

♠ A 10 4   ♠ 6 2
♥ A K 9 7 6   ♥ 8 4
♦ A J 5   ♦ K 4
♣ 10 2   ♣ A K Q J 9 7 3

After an opening bid of 1♥, responder bid 2♣, and then after 2NT he bid 5♣. It did not require a mathematical genius to see that there were 12 top tricks, and opener bid a slam that was almost universally missed.

If you read about the 'Crowhurst' convention in the relevant chapter you can see how fluently and easily it can be incorporated into almost any method, and how it lends itself to a much more accurate exchange of information. Because of its invention, however, there is a wide school of thought that the 1NT rebid should now carry a wide range, in fact anything from a bare minimum opening bid up to 16 points. The advantages claimed are that one need never open 1NT with a hand that looks unsuitable, for instance a balanced hand with a small doubleton in one suit.

No doubt this method has had its successes, but they don't readily come to mind among the many occasions that I have played against this style. However, I can recall many incidences of waffling sequences when a balanced 13 point hand has chosen to open one of a suit and has then had the problem of unscrambling the subsequent auction. I suppose that, in theory, to open 1NT with balanced hands of all types can sometimes lead to the wrong contract, but it doesn't happen very often in practice. I have many times, at the table, been heard to say 'Another triumph for the weak no-trump', when a hand such as the following has turned up:

♠ K 6 3 2   ♠ Q 8 4
♥ K 10 9   ♥ J 3
♦ 10 5 2   ♦ A K 8 3
♣ Q 8 4   ♣ K 10 7 4

West	East
—	1♦
1♠	2♠

Result: minus 200.

The 1NT overcall has remained fairly standard for many years, in keeping with its sound logical base. An immediate overcall should show something in the region of 16—18 points, should be balanced and have a guard in the opening bid suit. Sometimes with a hand such as the following, though not ideal, a 1NT overcall has less defects than any of the alternatives. After an opening 1♥ bid 1NT on:

♠ A 10   ♥ K Q 4   ♦ A Q 10 7 6 2   ♣ Q 7

It is a 1NT overcall in the protective position that leads to much more controversy and, certainly, much less efficiency. The vast majority of players still insist that the protective bid of 1NT, for instance 1♥—Pass—Pass—1NT, should show a balanced minimum hand, and that with 13 or more points you must double. It does not take much imagination to foresee the multitudinous problems that arrive from putting a strait-jacket on a player in the protective position. I quote a few hands and the problems that arose. What would you have done in each situation?

(a) ♠ K 10 4
     ♥ 8 3
     ♦ K Q 10 3   1♠   Pass Pass Dble
     ♣ A Q 7 2   Pass 2♥   Pass ?

(b) ♠ Q J 5 4
     ♥ A J 7
     ♦ A Q 4 2   1♥   Pass Pass Dble
     ♣ 3 2   2♥   3♣   Pass ?

(c)   ♠ 6 2
       ♥ J 8 6 4 3
       ♦ J 4 2
       ♣ Q 6 3   1♥   Pass Pass Dble
                  Pass 2♥   Pass 2NT
                  Dble ?

All led to calamity and none would have presented any difficulty
had the re-opening 1NT had a little more flexibility.

There is no ready-made success method available. Always in
some area there will be a great deal of slack to be taken up and it
seems sensible to me that the area of the greatest slack should be
at the lowest possible level. I would strongly recommend that the
protective 1NT should show a fairly wide range, say 11—16 points.
Before you recoil aghast at the thought, let us examine the implications. After one of a minor, and in particular 1♣, is passed to you
in the protective position, you need not bid 1NT with the higher
point range because a double will normally receive a response at
the one level and you can then rebid 1NT. But after a bid of one
of a major on your left, especially when vulnerable, this wide range
does solve a lot of very nasty problems. Suppose that the bidding
proceeds 1♠—Pass—Pass—, and you hold the following hand:

      ♠ A 10 4 2   ♥ 10 3   ♦ K J 9 4   ♣ A K 3

This hand cost us a big match when our opponents were able
to simply bid 1NT.

If your methods dictate that you must double, because you are
too strong to bid 1NT, what do you do next if partner bids 2♥? As
partner has to bear in mind that you will double on just any old
hand with 13 or more points, the 2♥ bid itself carries necessarily a
wide range. The corollary of having a wide range protective 1NT,
is that doubles will always show hands with good shape, or hands
that are too strong to bid 1NT.

Of course, with such a wide range, even at the lowest level, it
becomes efficient to incorporate a 'Crowhurst' type 2♣ inquiry

by responder to the protective 1NT. In simple style, I would suggest that after a 2♣ inquiry one should, with sights set on the most likely game, always bid a major if possible. After 2♣, 2♦/♥/♠ all show hands in the minimum range, while jump bids show five card suits and hands in the upper range. After 2♣, 2NT would show a hand in the maximum range, and it's for you to decide the break line and the ensuing method of investigating the best game.

One can now logically adopt a bid of 2NT in the protective position to show a hand with the values to rebid 2NT in a normal constructive sequence such as 1♣—1♥—2NT, i.e. 17—19 points. Again, a partnership should decide on the definitive machinery it should use afterwards.

When the protective bidder doubles and then bids no-trumps, his partner will always have some idea of his general high card strength. It is possible to get too high if one player protects with 1NT on a minimum hand, and his partner makes a game inquiry ending in a contract of 2NT with a combined 21—22 points. Although this seems unsound, in practical terms 2NT nearly always proves to be playable because of your knowledge of the distribution of the enemy high cards.

In discussing a 2NT bid from the 4th seat, one is reminded of an immediate 2NT overcall. Most players employ this bid as the so-called 'Unusual no-trump' to show both unbid majors or both unbid minors, whichever the case may be. For example, the bidding 1♠—2NT shows both minor suits and 1♣—2NT shows both major suits. I gave up this method many, many years ago and have never once regretted it. I cannot remember getting a bad result from not being able to use this very inefficient weapon.

To be efficient one would have to define so closely the playing strength and defensive values of the 2NT bidder that its frequency would be almost non-existent. When you give the bid greater latitude, responder is always in some doubt as to what action he should take. Then again, if responder only gives simple preference to one of your announced suits, it takes a great deal of heart-searching for the original bidder to decide whether or not to bid on, because while the responding hand might be ideal for game, it might also be entirely lacking in suitability, and disaster would then definitely ensue.

Another major disadvantage is that if the opponents finally play the hand, and that happens very often, you have presented declarer with a blueprint for his play. Contracts that would not succeed normally become double dummy by reason of your bidding. Meanwhile my team has had considerable success by having the 2NT bid available in its natural sense. Whilst in principle it shows something about the strength to open 2NT, it may sometimes be a little less strong with a near solid suit. The following hands would be ideal for a natural bid of 2NT over an opening 1♠:

(a)   ♠ K 10 4   ♥ K Q 6   ♦ A Q 9 8   ♣ A K 4

(b)   ♠ A 7   ♥ K 4   ♦ A K Q 10 8 7 ♣ Q 4 2

If you decide to remain faithful to your 'unusual' 2NT bids at least let me persuade you to use them to show any two suits, at least this will increase the frequency of use. If you stick with your usual treatment, I recommend the following definitive aid. It could also be used with Michael's cue bids.

Suppose the bidding starts 1♠–2NT–Dble, on your left. This normally shows that your opponents feel that they have you outgunned, and suggests that left-hand opponent can double you in at least one of your suits. Already you gain if your opponents do not know exactly which two suits are being shown. I now recommend that, if responder passes, for instance 1♠–2NT–Dble–Pass, this would show a hand with equal preference for both specified suits, if responder bids, such as 1♠–2NT–Dble–3♣, this would show a preference for clubs rather than diamonds but would guarantee at least two diamonds. If responder redoubles, 1♠–2NT–Dble–Rdble, this would guarantee a singleton in one of your suits. You would now bid the lower of your two suits and if that is partner's singleton he will rescue your side into its best strain. The following hand would be a good example:

♠ 10 7	♥8	♦ A 10 9 8 7	♣ A Q J 10 7
1♥	2NT	Dble	Rdble
Pass	3♣	Pass	Pass
3♥	?		

You now know that partner has a singleton diamond and you can readily see that, in keeping with the policy you have adopted of trying to be disruptive and aiming at sacrificing against a high level enemy contract, the knowledge that partner has a particular singleton or denies a singleton is of great value in helping you to make the right high-level decision.

Chapter 3.
Response

It is normally correct to respond with the longest suit first, just as it is normally correct for opener to bid his longest suit first; after all a bid is a matter of suggesting a trump suit. As responder your keynotes are economy and forethought. You do not have to give a promise to carry on bidding as does the opener. Thus whereas opener with two four card suits would open one rather than another to facilitate a rebid, responder should bid the lower suit first so that opener, if he fits the second suit, will be able to show it at an economic level.

Sometimes though, with two four-card suits you are only strong enough to bid just once. Then common sense dictates that it is best to bid the strongest suit. If your partner opened 1♣ and you held:

♠ J 6 2   ♥ K Q 8 3   ♦ 9 7 4 2   ♣ 8 4

it would be more useful and efficient to respond 1♥ rather than a pedantic 1♦. I would do the same with a diamond more and a spade less. Transfer the heart and spade holdings and 1♦ becomes more sensible, because we retain economy and the spade suit is rarely shut out.

Increase the strength so that you intend to bid again, even after a minimum rebid by opener, and basic principles often seem to be discarded without rhyme or reason. Take the sequence 1♦—1♥/2♦—2♠; I would willingly bet that most natural bidders would claim that responder should have at least five hearts. But why? He has bid his two suits in logical order, and what is he supposed to bid with

♠ A K 8 3   ♥ A K 8 3   ♦ 8 3   ♣ 8 3 2

But when bids are not made in their logical sequence, such as 1♦—1♠—2♦—2♥, opener can then be sure that responder has at least five spades. This last example raises the point of whether or not responder's second suit is forcing. The tried and trusted methods say no, not when preference can be given at the same level. If you hold:

♠ K J 9 8 4   ♥ Q J 9 6 4   ♦ 2   ♣ 8 4

you would agree that you would prefer to play in 2♥ or 2♠ rather than pass 2♦.

It can be argued sensibly that to regard the second suit as forcing only loses on low level part scores and gains on the hands where you need to develop the auction. Another advantage is that if 2♥ is forcing in this sequence, then 3♥ can be used to describe a different hand type, perhaps a game forcing major two-suiter, perhaps a control with diamond agreement on a hand such as:

♠ A Q 9 7 3   ♥ A 4 2   ♦ K 10 2   ♣ 5 3

You might even be able to combine both possibilities, and this is for partnerships to decide.

But a decision must be made, and the implications of the decision must be discussed. All agree that if responder's second suit is a reverse, then the bid is forcing. Thus if the bidding proceeds 1♦—1♥—2♦—3♠ the jump is unnecessary In keeping with our style, which seeks to create as many parallel situations as possible, this extravagant use of space has a specific meaning. In principle it agrees diamonds and shows a spade control. It could, for instance, be

♠ A K 4   ♥ A 10 9 8 7   ♦ Q 6 4 2   ♣ 8

when the intention is to play in no-trumps if possible. Or it could be:

♠ A 7   ♥ A 9 7 6 3   ♦ K 8 7 3   ♣ A 4

when a slam is not far off facing a suitable minimum opening bid.

Should responder have a powerful major two-suiter with longer hearts than spades there is no reason why the bidding should not proceed 1♦—1♥—2♦ —2♠—?, and then a heart or spade rebid would show responder's distribution.

One problem that responder has to deal with from time to time is whether or not to make an immediate game force after partner's opening bid. Going back to the earliest days of natural bidding, the object of a game force is to suggest to opener that the combined assets might well lead to a slam facing a minimum opening, provided that there is a good fit. It is obviously of great comfort for a partnership to know that game at least is a sound proposition, and that a slam can be investigated from an early level.

The accuracy of the final contract is going to depend on the accuracy of the exchange of information, and this is the fly in the ointment. The mere fact that you force means that you consume space. Should the suit that you wish to show be the one lower in rank than the opener's, the space consumed is quite considerable, and should you wish to show two suits the whole thing can become very unwieldy. Take a sequence such as 1♠—3♥—3♠—4♦, we are still below game, but there will be many hands where a lot yet needs to be discussed before the partnership can decide on its happy resting place.

Because of this, most players nowadays agree that after forcing, a suit bid at the four level is not natural but a cue bid agreeing opener's suit. The sequence 1♠—3♥—3♠—4♦ would show a hand such as:

♠ A J 6   ♥ A K Q 9 4   ♦ A 10 2   ♣ 4 3

Some go so far as to say dogmatically that they never force with two-suited hands. It seems silly to discard the solid and logical foundations of natural bidding just because some thinkers have discovered a more effective way of dealing with isolated examples. The passage of time has not altered the feeling of comfort that comes when both partners are aware of the slam potential.

It is also a considerable factor that in many cases a good auction develops when responder makes some very strong sounding bids under the cover of the knowledge that he was not strong enough to force in the first place. As in so many cases it is just a matter of looking ahead. If you can force and describe your hand to a fine degree of accuracy at an economical level then it must be right to force with the required values.

Strong one-suited hands are easy enough, because you can force and then rebid your suit. But if you held

♠ A K J 10 7   ♥ A K Q 10 8   ♦ 6   ♣ 7 2

it would be silly not to force with 2♠ after an opening bid of one of a minor, because you can bid your second suit at the three level. You are able to show both your hand pattern and your strength, and opener will know after the second round of bidding that minor suit aces are vital, and that lesser honours could probably be disposed of in the nearest waste bin. You have to jump sometime and to leave it until later could be too late i.e. 1♦—1♠—2♦—3♥—3NT—?

Another hand that needs to force in order to ensure any kind of intelligent discussion is the strong balanced hand. Holding for instance:

♠ A Q 8 7   ♥ K 8 3   ♦ A J 4   ♣ K J 10

it would be foolish not to force after an opening bid of 1♣/♦/♥. Assume that you bid 2♠ and opener rebids his own suit or bids a second suit of lower rank, it is now correct and accurate to bid 3NT. This point is often overlooked. It is vital, having chosen to force, that you tell opener on the next round, just what was your reason for forcing.

If the bidding goes 1♥—2♠—3♥, and you now either raise hearts or cue bid a minor, opener will assume that you forced because of a heart fit. With a big balanced hand this is not so; you forced because you had a strong hand in its own right and you would have forced over any opening bid. It is very obvious that all subsequent bidding is going to gain clarity from both sides of the table when your hand has been described in type and strength to within fine limits.

To sum up, a force is an attempt to convey to the opening bidder, that facing a suitable hand there could be a slam; and the reason for forcing is to make sure that both partners are on the same wavelength. This is obviously desirable, and one should force with the sufficient values whenever it is expedient. The exceptions are the two-suited hands that cannot be shown below the level of 3NT, and some hands that are just too strong to force.

If you held:

♠ A 7 2   ♥ K 6   ♦ A Q   ♣ A K Q 9 7 4

and your partner opened either 1♦ or 1♥ it would be unwise to force with 3♣. While it is true that you have shown a strong hand and a club suit, it doesn't take much imagination to see that at a fairly early stage you are going to run out of bids that have any meaning. Should you respond 2♣ no doubt opener will be puzzled by your subsequent actions, but once it becomes obvious that you were always heading for a slam, opener will realise that you were dealt one of those hands that could be more efficiently bid by asking rather than by telling.

Another advantage of not forcing is that you will hear from opener a natural, logical rebid. If, for instance, the bidding had started 1♥–3♣, then a 3♥ rebid by opener could be made on a minimum hand or a hand with extra values. Should the bidding start 1♥–2♣–2♥ at least you are in no doubt that partner has a minimum opening bid.

It is also strongly recommended that one should not force on a suit that is headed by a queen. Here again, you may be dealt with a very powerful hand such as:

♠ Q 10 9 8 3   ♥ A 4 2   ♦ A 4 2   ♣ A Q 4

and have the problem of dealing with an opening bid of 1♥. To force with 2♠ is the one sure way to get to a slam with two top spade losers, and even if you are lucky enought to avoid the lead, it is extremely unlikely that the two losers are going to vanish. So you may ask how one shows the strength of the hand after simply responding 1♠. Well, it is true that the auction will tend to sound odd to your partner, but once it is agreed that you will not force with a hand too strong to describe itself, nor when the only available suit is headed by a queen, your partner should have little difficulty in working things out at a later stage.

We all readily agree that in general terms, should partner open with one of a major suit we would like to be able to support immediately, thus solving future communication problems. We also take it as read that when playing a system that allows one to open with a four card major suit, responder would prefer to have four card support. However, hands do arise when to support immediately with only three card support seems to be the most sensible course. Holding, for instance:

♠ K 6 3   ♥ 4 2   ♦ K 8 4 3 2   ♣ J 10 2

and partner opens 1♠, there would appear to be a choice to describe your limited values with either 1NT to show 6—9 balanced points, or a raise to 2♠. There can be no doubt about the right bid and that is to support. If the matter could be summarised I would suggest that in all these areas of doubt, it is better to adopt a policy of always being in a contract that must be sensible. It is so very obvious that on this hand 2♠ can never be an idiotic contract; even if on occasions 1NT may be better, it cannot be said that this is true the other way around. A contract of 1NT could be quite ridiculous.

The next range of hands where one feels that perhaps the responding hand is just a little too strong to give immediate support often leads to amorphous sequences. Take as an example the hand:

♠ Q 10 8   ♥ 8 2   ♦ A Q 9 6 4   ♣ 6 4 2

and again partner opens 1♠. There are many that would argue that the hand is strong enough to respond at the two level. However, should you choose to respond 2♦ and opener then rebids 2♠, no-one would ever dream of bidding on and therein lies the problem. It is not difficult to construct minimum opening bids that will make game facing this responding hand and very often the crucial factor is the spade support. It could well be that had the bidding proceeded 1♠—2♠ partner, comforted by the knowledge that there was an adequate trump suit fit, for instance with a long spade suit, may well be prepared to make a try for game. Had the bidding proceeded 1♠—2♦—2♠—Pass, it is only in the post mortem that the partnership would realise that it has just missed a solid game. Again to quote a general principle, I would suggest that when holding adequate trump support it is always wrong to introduce a new suit at the two level after an opening bid of one of a major unless one has the strength to subsequently support partner's suit.

Even when responder does have the strength to both bid and support there is a common little snag that is often overlooked. Supposing that you were dealt with:

♠ Q 10 2   ♥ A 7   ♦ J 9 4 3 2   ♣ A 5 3

and partner opened 1♠. Unarguably you have the values to bid at the two level, e.g. 2♦ , and then if opener should rebid spades you are strong enough to make a game try by raising to 3♥. The trouble is that in making the game try you have asked opener to make the decision on whether or not to bid the game. On what is he supposed to base his decision? Should be hold a singleton diamond, and the matter be in some doubt, then for sure he will pass, and that is just the kind of hand that you would like to play in game. Unfortunately should he have a diamond holding such as Q—6—5 he may well regard this as a valuable asset and bid the game thinking that the hands fit well, whereas in fact the game will be a very bad proposition. In my own autocratic way I tend to take the decision myself on responding hands of this type on the basis that there is no way that the opener can intelligently and sensibly judge the best level. Place the ace of hearts in with the diamonds and one can see the difference, now you can respond 2♦ and raise a rebid of 2♠ to 3♠ knowing that the opener, whatever his subsequent decision, will be making his decision expecting the cards that you in fact hold and thus he is more likely to be accurate.

Chapter 4.
Responding No-Trumps

Because a particular bid may promise certain high cards, suit length or point count, it is often misused. It is easy to see the fallacy in thinking you can open 2♣ with:

♠ A K x   ♥ A K x   ♦ A x x   ♣ x x x x

just because the book says that an opening 2♣ should include five quick tricks. Nowhere is this back-to-front idea so evident as in no-trump bidding. How often have we heard the pained cry 'I bid 2NT to show I had 11 points'? In fact you should bid no-trumps only because it is felt to be the right denomination.

Most players detest hearing partner leap to 2 or 3NT after an opening bid. No wonder, when so often it is just a naive point count communication. There must be a right hand to show via a no-trump (the response of 1NT is just a garbage can bid when all others are worse). Bearing in mind the basic rule that we should try to choose a trump suit for preference, to bid no-trumps is to suggest abandoning the security of a trump suit.

So if it is to be sensible to jump in no-trumps, the loss of space must be compensated by the accuracy of the information exchanged. If responder has the overall strength to bid two or three no-trumps logic suggests that other bids could be made on the way. The no-trump bid could be made at some later stage, and this must be the right approach when a hand may lend itself to several possible final contracts.

It always bothers me when I make what seems to be a logical bid and get a ludicrous result. Partner opened 1♣ and I made the 'perfect' response of 2NT with:

♠ K 10 4   ♥ K 9 8   ♦ K 9 8   ♣ K 8 7 3

This was passed out and down two. Going to the fountainhead, Jack Marx, I gave him the hand expecting him to bid 2NT (3♣ is not in style) and to my surprise he chose to respond 1♦. The reason? Partner can be 4—4—1—4 and we should never respond 2NT with a poor guard in the suit in which opener may have a singleton. Sure enough partner was 4—4—1—4 with 13 points. The correct sequence was 1♣—1♦—1♥—1♠—2♠—3♣.

The use of the Baron 2NT response to show strong balanced hands often facilitates big hand bidding, and details of this system are shown in the chapter on conventional aids.

However, it is not always sensible to bid suits just to avoid the accusation of naivety that comes from leaping in no-trumps. The following hand, played in a major pairs final, is a classic example:

$$♠ A K 4 \qquad ♥ 7 6 3 \qquad ♦ K J 6 \qquad ♣ Q 8 5 4$$

Throughout the field most chose the 'normal' response of 2♣ to an opening bid of 1♥, and after a rebid of 2♥ opted for 3NT. It could be argued that responder should have raised to 4♥, but one must have a certain sympathy with 3NT because of the general hand structure, and the pairs scoring. The club bid did not stop left hand opponent from leading from A—J—10—x—x in clubs, and they took the first five club tricks. Partner's hand was:

$$♠ Q 7 3 2 \qquad ♥ A K Q 10 4 \qquad ♦ Q 10 5 \qquad ♣ 2$$

When my partner held the responding hand, he bid 3NT over my 1♥ opening. This bid systemically promised at least three card support for my major suit, as well as a balanced hand with guards in all the unbid suits. It was now very easy for me to bid the par contract of 4♥, for one of the very few plus scores in the field.

We should agree, therefore, that after an opening bid of one of a major, a response of three-no-trumps should show a hand with about 14 balanced points, and include three cards in the opening bid suit. After an opening bid of one of a minor, responder should always bid a major suit first if possible, and so a jump to 3NT would again show about 14 points, a balanced hand, and very probably a distribution of 4—3—3—3 with a four card minor. The same general principles are applied to a response, with about 11 points, of 2NT to an opening bid.

This arrangement is very efficient after a third-in-hand opening bid. We all learn in our cradles the merits of opening in the third seat with a hand which might be below the strength for a normal opening bid. It is obviously sound policy to open 1♠ with the following after two passes:

♠ K Q J 10 6   ♥ K 3   ♦ J 9 4   ♣ 10 6 3

particularly if the vulnerability is favourable. One would normally pass any suit response and feel that one is in a fairly sensible contract. If we agree that a jump to 2NT always guarantees three card spade support, then opener can rebid his five card suit knowing that there will be eight trumps in the combined hands.

Chapter 5.
Opener's Rebids

When we decide to use natural bidding we accept that the opening bid carries a wide range, both in value and distribution. The task is subsequently to close this range, and the key bid in most auctions is opener's rebid. If lucky enough one can make a limited bid i.e. no-trumps, support suit rebid, and the rest is up to judgement and definitive agreements.

When not so lucky a second suit is introduced. This still carries a wide range, while promising no more than a bare minimum opening, it might contain 18 points. There can be no argument about this, since opener must show a second suit. After all, the main object of bidding is to find the best contract, and this might be impossible if you fail to mention one of your suits, however weak you may be. Opener cannot leap around just to show plus values, and 18 points facing a minimum of 6 is still not enough for game, unless a good fit is found. Thus responder has to bear in mind that opener might be minimum, but should keep the bidding open in case he is maximum.

To regard a second suit as forcing would be to take a good principle too far. It might rarely lead to catastrophe, but that's just one of the injustices of bridge. It would often lead to a convoluted and strained sequence and a kind of 'I guess, you guess and then I guess if you've guessed right.'

Sometimes the choice of rebid is completely automatic; for instance when you can bid a second suit without raising the level of the bidding whichever of your two suits responder might prefer. When you are dealt two five card suits there will be no rebid problem if the suits are either touching or both black. Then if you open the higher of touching suits, or clubs with the black suits, you can show the other economically.

If you are dealt with two non-touching five card suits, i.e. spades and diamonds or hearts and clubs, it is a time honoured principle to kick off by opening the major suit. If you are strong enough, even after the inconvenient response that partners always seem to make, you can show your second suit in spite of having to commit yourself to making nine tricks.

If you abandon the principle for reasons of expedience, do so in the knowledge that you are abandoning a principle. With non-touching five card suits and minimum values, it may be necessary to rebid one suit and forget the other. This is the reasoning behind opening the major suit in the first place; if one suit cannot be mentioned, then let it be the minor suit.

Your judgement may lead you to opening the following hand:

♠ 6 5 4 3 2   ♥ 8   ♦ A K Q 10 9   ♣ K 9

with 1♦. If partner responds 2♣, you will feel a lot happier about rebidding the diamond suit than bidding spades twice, which would have been your fate had you opened 1♠ and had a response of 2♥. This is a matter of judgement but, as mentioned, is abandoning good principles.

Only recently my partner held

♠ J 8 7 x x   ♥ —   ♦ A K J x x   ♣ K Q x

and opted to open 1♦, fearing the almost inevitable heart response should he open 1♠. In fact I responded 1♠, and despite displays of great excitement and enthusiasm, there was no way, with the other hand, that I could ever bid what proved to be a good slam. That fifth trump made all the difference.

Having established that opener should not jump about just because he has a few extra points, let us try to unscramble some of the bad thinking that surrounds the bidding when opener should make a jump rebid.

After an opening one bid and a simple response, opener must jump to make a game force, i.e. bid 1♣—1♥—2♠. This forces responder to bid again, and should not be made lightly; after all, responder has promised very little. If he were so weak that he would have passed a simple 1♠ rebid that might conceal a good hand, you will rarely miss a good game and often avoid many that are ridiculous.

But there are hands when a force is essential. Sometimes you are lucky enough to have the force suit, but you might equally just have responder's suit and sufficient values for game opposite a minimum response.

The bidding on the following hands could start, 1♣ – 1♥ – 2♠,

(1)	♠ A K 10 3	♥ A 8	♦ 9 3	♣ A K J 10 8
(2)	♠ A K 4	♥ A J 7	♦ 4 2	♣ A K 10 7 3
(3)	♠ A 4	♥ K Q J 6	♦ 5 3	♣ A K Q 5 3

Some would argue that No. (3) could be better handled by bidding 3♠, to make it clear that you are too good to raise to four hearts, and have a spade control but two losing diamonds. Some would opt for the cue bid of 3♠ only with one spade more and a diamond less, guaranteeing a singleton diamond. Some prefer 3♠ to be a splinter bid showing a singleton spade; others prefer it to guarantee no possible spade losers. It is of importance only that partners agree on one specific treatment, and decide what to do with the other big hands that do not quite fall into their category.

As the game force can be made with a variety of hands, responder must proceed with some circumspection. It is first necessary to find out the cause for opener's excitement, and so responder should next make what is called an impetus bid. He must try to be descriptive without consuming space. For instance you hold:

♠ A 5 2   ♥ K Q 10 3   ♦ Q 6 3   ♣ 8 4 2

and the bidding goes 1♣ – 1♥ – 2♠ – ?. 3♣ would be misleading since partner would expect more than x–x–x. 2NT certainly describes the shape but not the values, while although 3NT would show the extra points, it would be foolish because it denies opener space for communication, and should show better diamonds. 3♦ is the 'impetus' bid, and nothing will now give us a problem. It is also important that we have given opener room to jump to 4♥ to show *primary* support, a vital piece of information if instead we held:

♠ A 5   ♥ A 10 8 4 2   ♦ A 7 3   ♣ 8 7 2

We would still opt for the 'probing' 3♦ to find out more about opener's intentions.

Make our hand weaker, with:

♠ Q 6   ♥ K J 8 7 2   ♦ J 8 4   ♣ 8 7 2

and the best bid is 3♥. We are not interested in a slam facing an opening one bid, but opener may want to know if we have five hearts. It is well worth spending some time on thinking out the best continuations after your partner has opened and then forced.

To continue with our auction, after 1♣—1♥—2♠—3♦ what would you assume if opener now bids 4♦? The natural interpretation is that partner holds clubs, spades and diamonds. But if so, he would surely have bid no trumps. He may well have felt it necessary at first to show you his very powerful opening bid but your bid of his short suit would certainly not encourage him to proceed above the logical 3NT game. So a bid of the fourth suit by opener after forcing should agree responder's suit, and show primary four card support, with no losers in the fourth suit.

At this point you may well be asking yourself if it is necessary to adopt new methods that are going to occur only rarely. However, if the pattern of thinking that goes through this book is adopted, you will find that most of these new bids can be logically interpreted, because the essence of the style is itself logical. Although the frequency of any one specialised treatment may be low, the frequency with which one of these more unusual sequences occurs during a match is quite high; and what is more important, the frequency of gain or loss on these hands is very high.

The more expensive the rebid, then the more explicit must be the information imparted. Sequences such as 1♦—1♠—4♣ or 1♥—1♠—4♦, clearly agree responder's suit, but take up a lot of room. So we don't want partner having to guess as to just what goodies are included in opener's whale. This almost pre-emptive jump should show:

- (a) — a good opening suit, bearing in mind that it is not strong enough for an opening two bid.
- (b) — good support for responder.
- (c) — no losers in the jump suit.
- (d) — two losers IN THE UNBID SUIT.

For those who use this wild jump as a splinter bid, what would you bid, after 1♦—1♠, holding:

♠ K J 10 7   ♥ 8 3   ♦ A K J 7 4 2   ♣ A

Splinter bids are only really efficient when the splinter is sure to be a singleton small card, making it possible for partner to infer that all your known high cards are in the other suits. Bearing in mind the amount of space consumed, it is inefficient if partner does not know the vital information of where your high cards are situated.

It is common knowledge that a jump to game in your own suit after a simple response such as 1♥—1♠—4♥ shows a hand that has been improved by the bidding. The reasoning is simple. If you can contract for ten tricks facing any random six points, why did you not open 2♥ which only promises eight tricks? After a two level response the issue is not quite so clear cut, because you are facing a slightly stronger responder. Nonetheless, if only to maintain a consistent approach, opener should have at least tolerance for responder's suit. One would bid 1♥—2♦—4♥ holding:

♠ 7   ♥ A K J 10 8 4 2   ♦ Q 2   ♣ A J 3

There will occasionally be some awkward hands but no system can cater for them all. Some players suggest that after a two level response, a jump rebid should be forcing i.e. 1♥—2♦—3♥. It would obviously help on some hands, but just as surely there would be others that would cause quite a problem, for instance with:

♠ Q 8   ♥ K Q 9 8 5 3 2   ♦ 6   ♣ K Q 4

I would like to feel that responder could pass on unsuitable minimum after 1♥—2♦—3♥. If 3♥ is forcing in your method then you are likely to choose to rebid 2♥. Perhaps this is where the fashionable idea that 'two level responses are forcing to 2NT' was born. It is then necessary to respond 1NT over 1♥ with a hand such as:

♠ 6 2   ♥ J 4   ♦ J 4 2   ♣ K Q 10 9 7 6

Now you have to insist that 1NT is forcing, and the clubs appear like shrinking violets, peeping out to see the sun sometime later in the auction. Perhaps because the 1NT response is forcing, they have to adopt five card majors so that there is a tolerable bail-out point at a low level. It all reeks of jerry building to me, bodging up the holes as they appear, but weakening another part of the structure at the same time.

At the table the last hand shown was bid

(a) The cavemen: 1♥−2♣−2♦−3♣
(b) The scientists: 1♥−1NT-2♦−2♥

of course at table (b) responder could, and probably should, have chosen the same 3♣ rebid.

My real argument for a pure treatment is that if no-trump bids are made on hands that look like no-trump hands, if all suit raises and all suit rebids are limited, if suit bids promise only four cards, we are well on the road to acquiring the rhythm necessary for good partnership method.

Similar logic would explain a sequence such as 1♣−1♥- 4♣. If you open a minor and after a one level response leap to four of your minor, it should mean:

(a) A limit bid (all same suit rebids are limited)
(b) A hand improved by a fit in responder's suit
(c) You are not afraid of bypassing 3NT.

A spectacular success in a match was achieved with:

```
     ♠ 8 7 6 3                ♠ A 9 5 4 2
     ♥ A                      ♥ J 6 4
     ♦ J                      ♦ A K Q
     ♣ A K Q J 9 8 6          ♣ 7 3
```

The bidding was, 1♣−1♠−4♣−4♦−4♥−6♣. It was spectacular because, just for a change, the inferior slam of 6♠ failed in the other room when the trumps broke 3−1 in accordance with the odds.

There is not much to discuss about no-trump rebids, but a couple of points are worth bearing in mind. Years ago in the 'British Bridge World', Peter Swinnerton-Dyer, a British international, stated that is is never a heinous crime to overbid or under-bid by the odd point, but that disaster comes if you basically mis-describe the character of your hand. The other point is that you rarely get into trouble with a less than ideal rebid of 2NT, because partner should always probe if a sounder contract appears possible. However a rebid of 3NT must always be sound, because there is no escape route.

After support there should be no problems in theory. New suit bids are forcing games tries, and no-trump bids are natural. How-ever, one inefficiently handled situation is 1♣ −2♣ −3♠. Most would assume opener to be at least 5−5. If this were the case, he could bid 2♠ and then rebid spades. A much more useful arrange-ment is to assume only four of the major to be sure, a strong four:

♠ A K Q 9   ♥ K 7 4   ♦ 6   ♣ K Q 10 8 7

You can even reach good games with a 4−2 fit.

Chapter 6.
Bidding after Passing

The problems of bidding after passing are like taxes, they are always with us. Some players adopt SNAP (strong no-trump after passing), so that after passing, a bid of 1NT over partner's opening bid shows a strong hand. It doesn't take much imagination to construct many weak hands where a response of 1NT would fit the bill, but then some other bid must be concocted.

Other players adopt the DRURY convention, allowing a passed responder to bid 2♣ conventionally to inquire whether or not opener had a full value bid. But if partner had opened before you had a chance to pass, you would make your natural response and, presumably, arrive in some sensible contract. It doesn't seem to make sense to distort and completely change the structure of natural bidding just because the deal happens to have started somewhere else.

With my partners I always arrange to forget that one hand has already passed. So the sequence 1♠–2♣ is just as natural and forcing if the opener is in the third seat as in the first. Of course, opener should always exercise his common sense, and knowing that his partner does not have the values to open the bidding, he can choose to pass in some sound part score. But it is important that opener does not take fright after opening light, and leave the partnership floundering in some ridiculous 4–2 fit.

You will now avoid the problems that arise when you have passed with 9 or 10 points on a hand such as the following:

♠ J 6   ♥ 7 5 4   ♦ Q 10 7 2   ♣ A K 8 4

Had your partner opened 1♠ first in hand you would happily have responded 2♣ and trusted in your bidding machinery to get you to the right contract. If you follow the same path when your partner opens third in hand you are not going to arrive at some nonsensical contract, and it pays to reserve the natural 1NT and 2♣ responses for their time honoured purposes.

I hope that my readers are past the stage that having passed, they feel they have to make some kind of jump bid just to show that they have a near opener. This old fashioned idea stems from panic, and unnecessary panic at that. Because if your partner opens the bidding and passes your simple response, even if you have 10–11 points, it is highly unlikely that you will miss a reasonable game.

Jump bids after passing should be reserved for hands that specifically agree opener's suit. This has, apart from the obvious definitive advantages, another one. For instance, should the bidding go 1♠–3♠ opener knows that responder's raise is with a hand within the prescribed range, but with no particular values in a side suit. Whereas had the bidding proceeded 1♠–3♣/♦/♥, responder would show a good raise to 3♠, specifying exactly where his high cards exist.

This would certainly ease the problems of opener in deciding whether or not to go on to game. In some cases it could even help in reaching good slams on minimum but well fitting values. The following hand from tournament play illustrates the point:

♠ A J 9 4		♠ K Q 7 5
♥ A K 10		♥ 7 6 2
♦ 8 6 5		♦ 9
♣ A Q 7		♣ K J 9 5 2

At the table East dealt and passed, and the full bidding sequence was:

$$1♠–3♣–4♥–4NT–5♠–6♠.$$

The bid of 3♣ showed a full weight raise to 3♠ with good values in the club suit. Opener's rebid of 4♥ showed slam interest, and pinpointed the solid heart controls, and by inference the diamond weakness. This was just what his partner wanted, and after a simple check on aces, the good slam was reached.

The sequence 1♠–3♣–4♣ might also get you to the slam,

especially if you agree with partner that a 'trailing' hand, bidding before an unlimited partner, should automatically cue bid a control without promising any particular plus values.

You should agree with your partner just what it is that is shown by a jump bid after passing. Some pairs insist that responder should have a good suit and not just values, but I suggest that it is far more frequent and useful to show specific values rather than necessarily shape. If you first pass and partner opens 1♥ when you hold:

♠ A K 7   ♥ K J 10 4   ♦ 9 7 3 2   ♣ 8 4

it strikes me that a bid of 2♠, showing a good raise to 3♥ with spade values, is more likely to be of use to your partner than if you have to wait until you are dealt with both values and length in the suit you jump in.

I think the same system should apply after an opening bid of a minor, because of the tremendous aid to the accuracy of big hand bidding by showing not only your general strength, but specifically where this strength is held. It really makes sense that the bidding should go 1♦–2♠ to show a good raise to 3♦ with a good holding in spades. It may enable the opener to bid no-trumps in comfort, and should a non-existent major suit be raised, responder can always retreat to the minor or perhaps try 3NT knowing that his partner has already been informed where his high card values lie.

Chapter 7.
Raises of Opening Majors

When a player opens one of a major, it is easy enough if responder has primary support and the strength to raise to only two or three. When responder has enough to feel that game is on, it is vital to differentiate between the many types of hand that can, for instance, raise 1♠ to 4♠. It is very helpful to use some kind of 'SWISS' machinery, using jumps to 4♣ or 4♦ to show specific types of balanced major suit raises. Details can be found in the chapter on conventional aids.

Another way of giving added definition is by use of the 'delayed game raise'. This is based on the premise that with genuine major suit support responder will always raise immediately. So if a sequence proceeds 1♠—2♣—2♦—4♠ opener, who has promised no more than four cards in his suits, will know that responder also has at least four spades. So it follows that the 2♣ bid was an attempt to show specific values in a particular suit en route to the spade support that was to come later.

It is important to stress that with a raise of 1♠ to 4♠, whether via 'SWISS' or with a delayed game raise, the overall strength, counting distribution, of the responding hand should be about the same irrespective of the approach. But there will, of course, be considerable differences between the various types of hand.

With a hand such as:

♠ A J 10 3   ♥ 2   ♦ 8 6 4   ♣ A Q 10 9 3

if partner opens 1♠, you begin by responding 2♣ with the intention subsequently of jumping to 4♠ to show your excellent support and good club suit. But sometimes the impetus is taken out of the intended jump by opener simply rebidding his suit, i.e. 1♠—2♣—2♠. Now a jump to 4♠ will not guarantee primary spade support and would certainly end the bidding.

Since there are many minimum but suitable opening bids that would produce a slam facing responder's hand, it is important to carry through the original intention of making a delayed game raise. This can be done by responder making an unnecessary jump at his second bid. The bidding should go 1♠—2♣—2♠—4♥, and this last bid would show a control in hearts, genuine primary support for spades, and the obvious overtones of a club suit worthy of mention.

Good hands still create certain problems; for example, if you held:

♠ J 10 6 4   ♥ A 6 3   ♦ 4   ♣ A Q J 7 3

and your partner opened 1♠ you would realise immediately its high potential. I hope to goodness that even if playing some form of Swiss to show two aces, a singleton and good spade support, you would not consider this hand suitable. When this hand occured an international player did in fact choose to adopt a 'SWISS' approach. My comment at the time was 'Letting some players loose with conventions is parallel to sending children out into the garden to play with cut-throat razors.' This hand has specific potential whereas Swiss should show potential in balanced hands.

Since we have control in both hearts and diamonds, a decision has to be made as to which control to show after 1♠—2♣—2♠. This is a matter of partnership arrangement, but my recommendation is always to show the control which includes length. This is in keeping with our general philosophy of making bids that are as descriptive as possible. It one first bids clubs and then jumps in hearts, it is easy for opener to get an accurate picture of your likely hand pattern.

There is an added bonus from this general approach when opener rebids his major suit. With:

♠ A J 4   ♥ 6   ♦ K 5 2   ♣ A J 10 8 6 2

you would respond 2♣ to an opening bid of 1♠, since the hand is a little under strength for a force. But if opener now rebids 2♠ the hand takes on quite enormous proportions, and you should next jump to 4♦. Opener will assume that you intended to make a delayed game raise in spades, but this is not likely to lead to any serious mishap when the three card support is so good and the overall texture of the hand so suitable for high level ventures.

Sometimes after an opening bid of one of a major the next hand will insert a double. Nowadays it is common knowledge that one should support to the limit, and if necessary stretch a little in the process. But I do not subscribe to the view that the bidding 1♠–Dble–2♠ in effect denies the ability to raise at all. It is probably more relaxed to say that with this sequence responder is showing that his raise to 2♠ is of the non-defensive type.

A natural response of 2NT after a double is superfluous, since a redouble would normally be used with a balanced hand of this strength, so it has become generally accepted that after an opening bid of one of a suit is doubled, 2NT shows a high card raise to three of the suit.

For some reason this principle has not been followed through by some partnerships, and I would suggest that whenever you have genuine support for opener's suit, then the sequence 1♥–Dble–2NT should show *at least* a raise to 3♥ and possibly more. Opener will assume a good 3♥ response, and if he simply rebids 3♥, he will show that he would have passed a raise to 3♥ without the double. If responder now bids game he is saying that he had a full high card raise to 4♥. And if he introduces another suit, he would show sufficient values for a slam try. You have uncluttered the auction by first guaranteeing a primary fit with 2NT e.g.

♠ 7 3		♠ A K 4 2	1♥	Dble	2NT	Pass
♥ A J 8 5 2		♥ K Q 10 9 6 3	3♥	Pass	3♠	Pass
♦ Q J 7		♦ A 2	4♣	Pass	6♥	
♣ A 8 6		♣ 4				

Another point of these sequences is that an immediate raise to game after a double, such as 1♥–Dble–4♥, shows a pre-emptive, distributional hand without many defensive values.

Chapter 8.
The Constructive Auction

There is always a problem as to what sequences are forcing. Though no comment of genius, if cannot be repeated too frequently that forcing means simply that partner must not pass. A statement that 'this is 90% forcing' is rubbish; either your partner's bid permits you to pass, in which case, however encouraging, it is not forcing, or it insists that you bid in which case, however weak your hand, it is forcing.

It is often claimed that the weakness of a naturally based system is the lack of a definitive range. But in fact all artificial systems also have bids that carry a wide range.

An opening bid of one of a suit is assumed to show approximately 13—20 points, and obviously there is still much to discover. The same is true with a simple change of suit response. A strong club system has a narrower range when the opening bid is not 1♣, and so it does gain in that area of high frequency with hands of less than 16 points. But there is an immediate loss because one of the suits, clubs, is lost, or can only be shown by a strained and convoluted auction.

The unlimited nature of new suit bids creates most of the problems in a natural system. But it can be argued that while good judgement and method are necessary, one can use a partnership acceptance of the wide range of values to introduce subtlety and flexibility into the exchanges.

Many players are still influenced by the Baron doctrine that all bids of an unlimited nature are forcing. This becomes very disconcerting when a bid has to be found and every intelligent instinct tells you to pass after a sequence such as 1♥—1♠—2♣. The last bid promises no more than a bare minimum opening, but it could also be close to a game force. I believe it is better to rely on responder's judgement than to jump in a second suit on any random 18 points, just because you are hag-ridden with fear that game will be missed.

It would be fair to say that even with the values to make a game forcing rebid, it would be more prudent not to jump in a second suit without some reasonable tolerance for responder's suit. Some rebids by opener show strength by definition such as a reverse. Some think that a reverse bid should be forcing, but this argument does not stand up to close scrutiny. With the sequence 1♦ —1♠— 2♥ we might have a 17 count facing 6. Unless the hands have an exceptional fit, it is foolish for the bidding to proceed if a tolerable spot has already been reached.

Take for example the following hands:

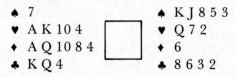

```
    ♠ 7                    ♠ K J 8 5 3
    ♥ A K 10 4             ♥ Q 7 2
    ♦ A Q 10 8 4           ♦ 6
    ♣ K Q 4               ♣ 8 6 3 2
```

No-one would want to bid on after 1♦ —1♠—2♥, unless they change the law to allow us to bid downwards. Here it should be stressed that although 2♥ is non-forcing, it nevertheless shows a good hand. Responder should try to keep the bidding open, especially if you bear in mind that even with 19 points opener will probably not bid 1♦—1♠—3♥ without some tolerance for the spade suit.

After a reverse, responder should take into account the announced values and beware of making a limited bid unless happy for opener to pass. After 1♦— 1♠—2♥, bids of 2♠ , 2NT and 3♦ would all show a minimum response, and are not forcing. At the risk of repetition, this means that opener can pass; it does not order him to. Obviously he would prefer that we have a point or two in hand rather than make a jump to what could be the second-best contract.

Jump rebids by responder are not forcing but are rarely passed, i.e. 1♦ —1♠/2♥—3♠ would show something like:

♠ K Q 10 9 5 3   ♥ 7 5   ♦ K 7   ♣ J 6 3

However after a reverse, jump preference for the first of opener's suits, or a simple raise of the second, are forcing. Consequently, jumps to 4♥ or 5♦ would seem to be unnecessary. As before, when such a bid consumes undue space, it is vital that the meaning is explicit.

Good bidding needs study and the ability to remember many treatments. Memory is fallible, and it is a help if a common denominator can be found to link a number of similar bids. One such is that unnecessary jumps should show hands of moderate value but high suitability. Thus we bid:

1♦—1♠/2♥—4♥ with

♠ A J x x x   ♥ K Q x x   ♦ x x   ♣ x x

and 1♦—1♠/2♥—5♦ with

♠ Q J x x x   ♥ x   ♦ K J 10 x x   ♣ x x

In the second example it would be unwise to make this jump if the hearts and clubs were reversed as partner will not expect a club control.

A reverse bid after a two level response is a different kettle of fish. Since a two level response requires a little more values, the combined minimum point count would normally be in the region of 25, after a sequence such as 1♥—2♣—2♠. It is now logical that the bidding can proceed further safely. Since a forcing situation is created, there are two more factors to bear in mind:

(1) It is no longer necessary for responder to jump for fear that opener may pass.

(2) Opener could very well choose to reverse into a second suit which has less than the normal requisite of four cards.

So the sequence 1♥—2♣—2♠ is forcing, and subsequent preference to 3♥ by responder is also forcing. So again we have an apparently superfluous bid of 4♥. In keeping with the philosophy already suggested, this would show a minimum hand but with ideal suitability.

A hand such as:

♠ J x   ♥ K x x   ♦ x x x   ♣ A J 10 x x

would be admirably described by this unnecessary jump to 4♥

after 1♥—2♣—2♠. If the responder had three card heart support with either additional strength or dispersed values, a simple bid of 3♥ would suffice. Over a 3♥ bid, it is essential that opener next either limits his hand, or makes a cue bid if he has either considerable plus values or immense suitability.

We have mentioned that in the sequence 1♥—2♣—2♠, opener might have had to bid 2♠ with only a three card suit, so generally responder will not jump to 4♠. Of course there are always exceptions, and this jump would certainly describe a hand such as:

♠ K J 10 9   ♥ x x   ♦ x x   ♣ A K x x x

very accurately. If opener has only three spades, responder has sufficient values to find some other playable spot, and opener will know this, and that it is a possible three card suit which has been raised to the four level.

In old fashioned Acol, a rebid of the same suit by responder was regarded not only as not forcing, but actively discouraging. Time has suggested that this is less than efficient. If the bidding commences 1♥—2♦—2♠, and you hold

♠ Q x   ♥ J x   ♦ A Q J 10 x x   ♣ x x x

it would be unfortunate if a simple rebid of 3♦ at this point were to be regarded as a complete sign off. It would be very difficult to convey a proper picture of the hand after some meander through the fourth suit.

If we opt for making the bid forcing, we also opt for the risk of playing at a level one too high. Generally if the bidding went 1♥—2♦/2♠—3♦/3♥—4♦, the last bid would simply be a pleas to be left in peace, and the contract would frequently prove to be playable. But if we have to balance the chance of being one off in a part score, against the efficiency and accuracy of constructive bidding in the game plus zone, it is not difficult to see which option gives the better chance for large gains.

To get back to the earlier sequences, when no early limited bid can be made in another suit. We do not have a problem, in general, when a suit is raised or when no-trumps are bid immediately. There may be a better way to communicate, but there are no problems of genuine definition.

We started the chapter with the sequence 1♥–1♠–2♣, so let's take it from there. If responder now bids 2♠/2NT or 3♣, a reasonably fine limit has been drawn, and the rest is up to your judgement, which hopefully will improve as your partnership develops an attitude of relaxation and clarity towards bidding. But equally there must be sufficient thought and knowledge to make sure that you do not miss the best contract.

With the sequence 1♥–1♠–2♣–2♥, 2♥ is not really a bid at all. It could be said that but for the happenstance that responder preferred hearts to clubs, 2♣ would have ended the auction. You must also remember that since opener has a fairly wide range, responder may want to give false preference to hearts in order to keep the bidding open. This does not mean that we should assume that there are always values to spare.

If responder is minimum with three card support for an opening major, he would often choose to raise 1♥ to 2♥ immediately. Thus when he bids 1♥–1♠–2♣–2♥, he will often have only two hearts. Alternatively, he might have a hand with five spades and three hearts, and feel that, as no space would be lost by introducing the spade suit, it would be silly to decide on a heart suit that may be 4–3, when spades could be 4–5.

Another common situation is when responder has genuine primary support for opener's second suit. He will then want to show this, and give more specific information about his hand's strength and type. After 1♥–1♠–2♣, a simple raise (if that is all the hand is worth) shows only limited values. But if responder is stronger, it is vital to express both the fit and the suitability. So let us examine the ways in which the second suit can be raised:

(a)   1♥–1♠–2♣–3♣
(b)   1♥–1♠–2♣–4♣
(c)   1♥–1♠–2♣–5♣
(d)   1♥–1♠–2♣–2♦–?– club support
(e)   1♥–1♠–2♣–2♦–?– Jump club support
(f)   1♥–1♠–2♣–3♦–?–

Let us define these alternatives in line with our overall bidding philosophy. The jump to 4♣ can be logically interpreted, as having considerable distributional assets, since we have by-passed 3NT. Is it forcing? I suggest not, as a parallel to similar jump raises, and because there are other ways of supporting clubs and retaining a forcing situation.

The sequence is exactly parallel to 1♠—2♣—2♥—4♥; in other words a seven loser hand with good support, that has no inclination to play in no-trumps, and expects to make ten tricks. Opener would almost see the 5—5 distribution facing him.

The jump to five clubs is even more space consuming, and so must be even more specific in its description. It is obvious that the hand has violent distribution, but the bid leaves the opener no way of finding out if responder has the right cards to make a slam. So its use should be restricted to a specific hand that, in effect, tells opener to bid six if he has two aces. A typical example would be:

♠ A K x x x x   ♥ x   ♦ x   ♣ K Q x x x

Once we start on the fourth suit sequences we are getting into areas where the edges are blurred. In a sense the very lack of clear outlines should give opener an idea of responder's hand, since he knows his partner does not indulge in convoluted manoeuvres just to make the bidding interesting. Opener assumes, to start, that a bid of the fourth suit is a general request for more information, and opener should make what he considers to be the bid which best describes his hand.

As we shall see in the chapter on fourth suit bidding, if responder next supports either of opener's suits, this is forcing. It may be that responder is still in doubt as to the right strain, so after 1♥—1♠/2♣ —2♦/2♠—3♣, there may still be possibilities of playing in hearts, spades, clubs or no-trumps. Obviously responder has ambitions, at least to the game level, and may possibly even be starting a slam investigation.

If simple support after the fourth suit is forcing, we meet yet again the unnecessary jump. Sticking to our guidelines, we can logically interpret this jump as having at least game values with guaranteed working cards. The following hand from an inter-county match demonstrates this point:

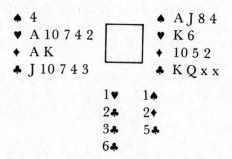

♠ 4	♠ A J 8 4
♥ A 10 7 4 2	♥ K 6
♦ A K	♦ 10 5 2
♣ J 10 7 4 3	♣ K Q x x

1♥	1♠
2♣	2♦
3♣	5♣
6♣	

Opener was in no doubt when bidding the slam.

Had responder held:

♠ K Q x x   ♥ Q x   ♦ J x x   ♣ K Q x x

he would simply have made a forcing raise to 4♣. So the guarantee of working cards meant that the spades had to be headed by the ace, since the king-queen would bewaste paper opposite a single-ton. The hearts had to be king doubleton, since that is a holding that is guaranteed to have working value; queen doubleton could so easily mean an inescapable loser. There is also a very clear infer-ence that responder has two losers in the fourth suit.

After 1♥—1♠—2♣, with two diamonds forcing, three diamonds must agree clubs and also show a diamond control. It is much more flexible to define as a control a holding in which the opposi-tion cannot take the first two tricks, i.e. ace, king or singleton, rather than restrict its use to a guarantee first round control. There is always plenty of time to establish first round controls, but unless at some stage someone makes a bid that is both definitive and descriptive, the whole auction will develop an ever increasing haze.

How about sequences that start 1♥—2♣ — 2♦ in which the re-sponse and opener's change of suit are both at the two level. Many top players now regard this sequence as forcing, and although this has no real basis in mathematical logic, it has a high degree of efficiency in practice. I think the Sharples twins sum it up well by saying that this bid is not forcing, but as you have not passed in the last thirty years why the blazes should you start now? It might be as well to mention here that while it is not exactly desirable for partnership confidence, it is much less important that a player chooses to pass a bid he knows to be forcing, than it is for him not to know it was forcing in the first place.

If we start with the basic premise that after a two level response a change of suit will be regarded as forcing there is more scope to bid accurately certain awkward hands of indeterminate range. Take for example:

♠ x x   ♥ A K x x x   ♦ A Q x   ♣ K x x

After 1♥—2♣ there is no really accurate bid available, and it is best to use a flexible 2♦ bid to allow the conversation to develop logically. So if once every few years partner opts to pass the forcing bid of 2♦ (a) it means that he probably didn't have the values to bid 2♣ in the first place and (b) these sequences do lead to some very interesting play problems.

Chapter 9.
Fourth Suit and After

So much scientific abracadabra has been attached to a bid of the fourth suit that it has almost developed a mystique. The average player approaches the subject with a feeling of awe that is not surprising when even better players talk of it as if it were a highly technical part of the expert's vocabulary.

To put it simply, a bid of the fourth suit is forcing and often the only forcing bid available. It neither promises nor denies any particular hand, but suggests that it has been used because no other simple, accurate description of the hand could be found.

Years ago, one of the world's greatest players described the use of the fourth suit as 'a pitiful crutch'. Even he was forced to accept the logic of the efficiency of this 'new' treatment, in terms of frequency of usefulness. With the sequence 1♥—1♠—2♣—2♦, is it not unlikely that responder is still trying to find the best strain? Of course responder can often give preference or bid no-trumps in order to lead to a good contract. But, after 1♥—1♠—2♣, what can responder sensibly bid with:

♠ A Q 7 4 2   ♥ 10 3   ♦ J 4 2   ♣ K Q 5

Hearts? Clubs? Spades? or No-trumps?

To get to the right spot without inspired guesswork, we need to keep the lines of communications open, and this can only be achieved by responder making an unlimited, forcing bid, and 2♦ is the most economical one that meets the requirements.

There is a lack of relaxation about the approach of players to the fourth suit. There is the unsophisticated view that the bid asks partner to bid no-trumps with the suit guarded, and that the parrot opposite should either bid no-trumps or deny a guard by making other noises. To be sure, one of the likely reasons for a fourth suit bid is to check on a NT guard, but the bid may be made for one of many reasons, and paramount should be the feeling that it asks for information. To reduce its use to a simple request for a no-trump guard is to discard many of the uses of one of the most flexible and comprehensive aids to definitive bidding.

One of the inherent dangers of having such a gadget available is that it might be used, just because it is there. The 'pitiful crutch' description becomes apt if the bid is employed to avoid, temporarily, the chore of thinking. As the bid of the fourth suit is a method of continuing a conversation without saying anything positive, the message is that responder wants to go on but is not sure of the right path.

Even an expert feels more at ease in dealing with the sequence 1♥–1♠–2♣–2NT, rather than 1♥–1♠–2♣–2♦. The first is unequivocable, while the second, though promising no more in terms of values, can conceal many intentions, including some infrequent exotica.

The most likely of the problem hands are those when responder has the values for no-trumps, but no ideal holding in the unbid suit. 'Most likely' does not mean certain. If you answer a request to give the best description of your hand, you do not bid 2NT with the following hand after 1♥–1♠–2♣–2♦,

♠ 6 4   ♥ K J 10 9 3   ♦ A 7   ♣ K J 10 2

Many top players did bid 2NT in a tournament, but surely 2♥ is a much more suitable description of the hand? It stresses the quality, places the hand in minimum range, and should it transpire that 3NT is the correct resting place, there is time enough to get there.

♠ 6 4		♠ A K J 5 3
♥ K J 10 9 3		♥ A 7
♦ A 7		♦ 10 6 3
♣ K J 10 2		♣ Q 9 4

Whilst most accepted the 3NT contract as part of the occasional inefficiency of any system, one pair bid 1♥–1♠–2♣–2♦–2♥–3♥–4♥ and looked, bewildered, at the score slip which showed them alone in collecting a plus score.

After introducing the fourth suit, responder is allowed to pass any limited bid by opener such as 1♥–1♠–2♣ –2♦–2♥/2♠/2NT/ 3♣. Because of this, some openers jump around as if they had been stung. Just because responder is allowed to pass does not mean that he often will. Some argue that if responder bids the fourth suit, he should guarantee to bid again. But this would mean that a minimum opening bid facing an awkward 10/12 points would have to reach uncomfortable levels. However, in accepting that opener must take responsibility for ensuring that things do not grind to a halt, it is not necessary to get over-enthusiastic just because there is a point or two to spare. What you lose by missing the occasional close game, you more than gain by the extra space for definition and a more controlled approach.

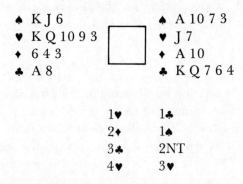

♠ K J 6	♠ A 10 7 3
♥ K Q 10 9 3	♥ J 7
♦ 6 4 3	♦ A 10
♣ A 8	♣ K Q 7 6 4

1♥	1♣
2♦	1♠
3♣	2NT
4♥	3♥

The contract of 4♥, so much superior to 3NT, was reached in relaxed style. East chose to show a minimum opener with a diamond guard by bidding 2NT. West was then able to make the well-chosen, delicate probe of 3♣ and, in view of the uncertainty of the final contract, East was not going to insist dogmatically on no-trumps, but chose instead a well-judged bid of 3♥, leading to the best contract. Those who bid 3NT over 2♦ would be sure to be in game, but far from sure that it was the correct game.

It follows that 3♣ was forcing. This situation is rarely fully discussed by partnerships. As suggested before, if after bidding the fourth suit, responder next supports one of opener's suits, this is forcing. (*1) But if responder rebids his own suit, then this is non-forcing, although it does not mean 'please pass'. It announces that opener, bearing in mind responder's own strength, can call it a day.

For example 1♥—1♠/2♣—2♦/3♣—3♠ can be passed. Responder has obviously six or more spades, but did not choose the simple path of 1♥—1♠—2♣—3♠. He therefore shows around opening bid strength. But two hands of minimum opening bid strength do not always produce a sound game, and if our method provides accurate information regarding the values and distribution, common sense will dictate the final decision. (*2)

As the fourth suit is forcing, a jump must have a special meaning. Sticking to our style, common sense suggests that 1♥—1♠—2♣—3♣ agrees clubs, and also shows a control in the fourth suit. One can see many ways of using fourth suit bids and jumps to give opener a real idea of responder's hand in the chapter discussing the methods of supporting opener's second suit.

What about such hands as:

♠ K 6   ♥ K 9 7 6 5 4 3   ♦ A 5   ♣ Q 4.

After 1♣—1♥—1♠, does a non-forcing bid of 3♥ make you feel the peace of mind that comes from a good bid? So we start with 1♣—1♥—1♠—2♦, and over 2NT we all agree that we want to rebid the hearts. If 3♥ is forcing, we could end up with the sequence 1♣—1♥/1♠—2♦/2♠—3♥/3NT, and do you then toil on with 4♥? But if

---

(*1) One could make an exception when opener has consistently told of minimum values that may be unsuitable. For instance 1♥—2♣—2♦—2♥—2♠—3♣. That is for partnerships to decide. You may sensibly opt to have no exceptions to the rule, and thus less memory strain. It would certainly be wrong to regard 1♥—1♠—2♣—2♦—2NT—3♣ as non-forcing, for although the 2NT bid promises no more than the barest opening bid strength, it will never show the kind of hand that screams danger because of a complete misfit. Also remember that opener may have a little to spare, preferring not to jump, to allow responder an extra round of bidding to help find the best game.

(*2) Some players assume all bids to be forcing after the fourth suit. They would argue that in sequences such as 1♣—1♥/1♠—2♦/2NT—3♥, the final bid must be forcing as responder could have chosen to bid 1♣—1♥/1♠—3♥. We all agree on the merits of this latter bid being limited, and that it should logically show a good heart suit.

3♥ is non-forcing and partner passes knowing that earlier·we had available the heart rebid and some other forcing bids, are you really worried about missing a good game?

One of the hands quoted earlier appeared as a bidding problem in *Popular Bridge Monthly:*

♠ K J 6   ♥ K Q 10 9 3   ♦ 6 4 3   ♣ A 8

After the sequence 1♣ −1♥−1♠−2♦−2NT, most experts were uncomfortable in accepting that 3NT was correct. Votes were cast for 3♠, forcing, arguing that it must show three good spades and general concern about the right game, but it might show four spades. Some went for 3♥, specifying it as forcing. Even if we accept that, will partner choose the right game for the right reason? The forcing bid of 3♣ solved all the problems, while even if 3♥ were forcing it simply passed on the onus to a partner who had limited information. He could not know about the good spades or the vital top club.

THE RAISE OF THE FOURTH SUIT

While some partnerships agree that a raise of the fourth suit is natural, it is obviously inefficient in terms of frequency. When a hand such as:

♠ 9   ♥ K Q 9 4   ♦ A J 6 3   ♣ K 10 7 3

comes along and the bidding begins 1♠−1♠/2♣ −2♦, you are delighted if your methods allow you to raise to 3♦ to show this hand. However, since the 2♦ effort often conceals a hand with a problem, you will finish in 3NT, and unless responder has full game values this will prove an uncomfortable spot.

Then again, if you are a little bit stronger, do you jump to 4♦? Partner is going to turn pale green if he was aiming at 3NT. We must admit that a bid of 3♦ feels better than the alternative of 2NT, but even so, diamonds will be the right strain only if partner is genuinely two suited. In this case, he must be strong enough to cope with a variety of inconvenient jump bids you might have chosen, so the diamond market can still be explored later.

So we decide to treat a raise of the fourth suit as a bid of a forcing, undefined nature, losing a little but gaining a lot. You gain in the space obtained in describing the stronger hands, the game-plus areas where accuracy leads to big profits. Some top players argue that a raise of the fourth suit should not only show considerable plus values but also a top honour in the fourth suit. Others prefer that the raise simply denies any accurate alternative. All agree that it should show at least an ace better than a minimum opening bid – for example:

♠ K 4   ♥ A J 8 3 2   ♦ K 3   ♣ A K 10 5,

when an elephantine leap to 3NT would remove all chance of getting to a possible slam.

There is one important exception to this rule. An opener with a 4–4–1–4 shape would start with 1♣ and rebid 1♥ over 1♦. If a spade fit is to be found, responder must bid 1♠ not only as a fourth suit probe, but also to be sure not to miss the best contract. Thus, 1♣–1♦/1♥–1♠/2♠ is natural and non-forcing, and if opener is stronger he should bid 1♣–1♦/1♥–1♠/3♠. This is a comfortable enough level facing either a minimum with a spade suit, or the 10 plus points that responder would have to use the fourth suit.

Chapter 10.
Opening Two Clubs

The corner stone of the original ACOL system was the opening two bids. Evolution has increased their efficiency, but the original concept remains.

What would you bid with:

♠ —   ♥ A K Q 10 x x   ♦ A   ♣ A K J 10 x x

If, like most, you open 2♣, then you are without sympathy for the philosophy of opening two bids which I shall hopefully, impart to you.

The essence of an opening 2♣ bid is the need to ensure that the bidding is given time to develop; that an intelligent conversation can ensue. There is no reason why the conversation should not then proceed along old familiar paths. Once again, the keynote is relaxation.

The 2♦ negative response speaks for itself. In economic fashion, the partnership has announced on one side a very powerful hand, and relatively little except gratitude on the other.

Most players seem to assume that when the opening 2♣ bidder next bids a suit it promises some mighty holding. In fact the sequence 2♣ –2♦–2♥ should show a suggested trump suit in exactly the same way as an opening bid of 1♥. Of course, on balance, suits bid after 2♣ tend to be more substantial than opening one bids but unless it is accepted that four card suits can be introduced on big balanced hands, contracts will tend to be bashed rather than bid.

Take, for instance, the following hand which helped one top team to eliminate another in a major competition:

```
          ♠ J 8 2                    ♠ K Q 4
          ♥ 9 8 7 2   ┌──────┐       ♥ A K 10 6
          ♦ A 6 4 3   │      │       ♦ K 10
          ♣ 8 4       └──────┘       ♣ A K 7
```

In one room the bidding was:		In the other room:	
West	East	West	East
—	2♣	—	2♣
2♦	3NT	2♦	2♥
Pass		4♦*	4♠
		6♥	

* cue bid agreeing
hearts

Guess which team lost?

Naturally it is essential in adopting this fluent and natural style that one is not too precipitous in supporting suits until it has been established that they have some length.

The old fashioned requirements for a positive response, while efficient *per se*, occurred with about the same frequency as Haley's comet. It is common sense that top cards have great importance and random minor honours are of nebulous value, so we cannot increase the frequency of positive responses simply on a point count basis.

The tried and tested Sharples method of positive responses over 2♣ is (a) 8 or more points including two kings or one ace, (b) a major suit as good as K–Q–J–x–x or K–Q–10–x–x–x, (c) the pristine 1½ tricks or more.

In passing, I should mention that it is essential to make a positive response when having the necessary requirements, with the rare exception of the time when you are so strong that you intend to bid a grand slam as soon as you have decided on the right strain.

A 2♣ opening bid requires five quick tricks, or more quick tricks than losers. This does not mean that if you have five quick tricks you open 2♣, but that if you open 2♣ you have five quick tricks.

When a 2♣ bidder has heard a positive response, to use the standard 4NT Blackwood responses subsequently is of dubious value. Facing a negative it is patently useless. To link with our three types of positive, if the 2♣ bidder opts to bid 4NT, the responses should be as follows:

After a negative response (2♦)	5♣	=	No kings
	5♦	=	1 king
	5♥	=	2 kings
	5♠	=	1 ace
	5NT	=	1 ace and plus values.

You will note that when responder makes one of the higher replies you will know that the hand contains less than eight points.

After a positive response	5♣	=	1 king
	5♦	=	2 kings
	5♥	=	1 ace and plus values
	5♠	=	1½ quick tricks
	5NT =		2 quick tricks.

After deciding that responder should make a positive bid, the choice of which bid is simple if you stick to the same style of simple constructive bidding. However, because of the trap of introducing bad suits on strong hands, we must be a little more strict on 'biddable' suit requirements; a minimum of three points in a four card suit suggests itself as reasonable. Thus 2♣ −2♥ would show a positive with at least four hearts that include three points. 2♣ −2♥ −2♠ would likewise only promise a four card suit, though on a frequency basis there will be more.

The 2NT response to 2♣ should always include the positive values previously mentioned, and would deny a biddable major suit. The common practice of responding 2NT just to show a certain point count helps only to create the fog that surrounds big hand sequences.

A young player once approached Bob Sharples with a hand, and asked what he should bid after opening 2♣ and receiving a response of 3NT. Bob replied: 'I'd enquire the time of the next train out. I would not wish to finish the session with an idiot who wasted the time needed to discuss the hand.'

Some jump bids are useful i.e. the time honoured jump in a suit:- 2♣–3♥ showing a solid suit such as A–K–Q–J–x–x or A–K–Q–x–x–x–x. This idea can be extended, so that a double jump would show a one-loser suit with no outside values. The following hand in a major pairs championship led to only one plus score, and that was only achieved because West gave up the unequal struggle. The bidding was too appalling to mention:

♠ A K Q J 10 7 5	♠ – – – –
♥ A Q 2	♥ 10 7 4 3
♦ A 10 4	♦ J
♣ – – – –	♣ A Q J 10 9 6 4 2

Along the lines mentioned this is a baby problem: 2♣–5♣–6♣.

There are some schools of thought that suggest that these semi-solid suits can be shown by first making a negative and then jumping. This is unnecessary and wasteful. Instead, after a negative response all jump bids by responder agree opener's last bid suit. The jump will show a control, ace, king or singleton. Voids are better shown by a double jump.

Chapter 11.

Opening Bids of Two of a Suit

Let's start by assuming that we are not going to employ 'Weak Twos' which, in my opinion, are not efficient unless allied to some kind of multi-purpose bid. We have already examined the opening 2♣ bid with its philosophy of setting the scene for an easy communicative auction. If the principle of the other opening two bids could be put into simple terms, it would be to say that far from wishing to discuss, opener wishes to inform. In other words the opening 2♣ sets the scene for a conversation to take place with a mutual exchange of information, whereas an opening bid of 2♦/♥/♠ suggests to responder that he should sit and listen, and then decide if his values are likely to be of any real use to the common cause.

Take for example the hand that we used to start the discussion of the bid of 2♣. When it occured in a top class team match the bidding at one table started 2♣, left hand opponent at favourable vulnerability bid 2♠, responder passed and the fourth hand bid 6♠. Opener, unfortunately, had shown nothing other than a strong hand. He opted to take a dip at 7♥. He had twin motives; firstly the contract could well be lay down, and secondly it was unlikely that the opponents would allow him to play in 7♥ when 7♠ was known to be relatively cheap, and so he would at least gain the maximum penalty. Unluckily the hand on his left, apart from sundry values in spades, had J—9—x—x in hearts, and doubled to avoid an unnecessary sacrifice. Dummy went down with:

♠ Q x x   ♥ x   ♦ J x x x   ♣ x x x x x

and so with 7♣ lay down, declarer conceded a 200 penalty.

In the other room the opening bid was 2♥, and although the enemy were not as ebullient in their competition, one could readily see that if the bidding had gone 2♥–2♠–Pass–6♠, now 7♣ would be a reasonable gamble. As it was 7♣ was allowed to play because left hand opponent had a certain heart guard, an ace and what could be a trick in diamonds, and hoped that the grand slam would fail.

One could create many examples of hands of this type. If for instance you held

♠ –   ♥ A K Q J 10 x x   ♦ K Q J 10 9 x   ♣ –

the hand would be completely described by opening 2♥ and over partner's response rebidding 6♦. Responder would now know that any black cards could be safely deposited in the nearest waste paper bin, but if he only held the diamond ace there would be thirteen tricks available.

If we are to have good constructive bidding sequences after an opening two bid, they must be forcing. The original idea of the ACOL two bid, was to make sure the bidding did not die, as it might if one had opened 1♥ and partner had a perfectly logical pass. However, time seems to have watered down the essential requirements for an opening two bid; perhaps I am a little pedantic, but with

♠ A K Q 10 x x   ♥ A x   ♦ A x   ♣ x x x

it would never cross my mind to open 2♠, although the odds suggest that there are eight tricks available. My reasoning would be that there is nothing in the hand to develop, it would require two definite tricks from partner before any game was likely, and in that case he would respond to an opening bid of 1♠.

Some players have the idea that to make a positive response requires the same high card values as a positive response to an opening 2♣ bid. This is not only inaccurate but inefficient. If responder feels he has sufficient values to make game, he should make a positive response on any hand that is likely to produce enough tricks. Obviously responder must use his common sense, as he will always have a second bid, and it would be unwise to over excite opener unless there was some genuine ambition beyond game.

The old-fashioned negative of 2NT is obsolete, and the Herbert negative style is fast becoming the norm, because of its increased efficiency. However there appear to be two schools of thought about how the bidding should proceed after a Herbert negative. The system of Sharples, Marx, etc., is that after an opening 2-bid, the next denomination should be the negative response, and that if opener then rebids no-trumps, he shows six of the opening bid suit and four of the next suit up.

For example, with:

♠ A K x x　　♥ A K Q 10 x x　　♦ x x　　♣ x

bid 2♥–2♠(Neg)–2NT – to show four spades and six hearts.

This enables responder to sign off in 3♥ or 3♠ or, if reasonable, to bid game in either suit. Those who argue that the 2NT bid should be treated as natural will find that generally opener can get across a no-trump hand by a jump to 3NT.

The advantages of this method are great. For instance in the old-fashioned style, with four spades, five hearts and a very powerful hand not sufficiently good enought to commit itself to game by opening 2♣, it was not possible to show both suits and stop before game. Now one can open 2♥ with this hand and over a 2♠ negative rebid 2NT showing four spades and, partner will presume, six hearts, thus giving you a certain degree of safety while not taking the dangerous risk of missing game althogether.

There is a second advantage, because if the bidding proceeds 2♦–2♥(Neg)–3♥, opener would be known to have six diamonds and five hearts and this is no small advantage when the premium on accurate bidding of big hands is so high.

If responder has a positive response, and wants to bid the suit that has been utilised as a negative, he should respond 2NT. For instance 2♥–2NT shows a positive response with a spade suit, and 2♦–2NT shows a positive response with hearts. With any other positive response the bidding can proceed quite naturally. Over a negative response we are able to bid hands with four spades and six hearts without getting too high, but if the bidding proceeds 2♥–3♣/♦, opener will then be content to show the spades naturally in the knowledge that the combined hands have at least the values needed for game.

Let us examine the situation where opener starts with a two bid, hears a negative response and then bids a second suit. It this forcing? Many play all new suit bids as forcing, but there appears to be no logical reason why after a sequence 2♥–2♠(Neg)–3♣ responder, with a completely unsuitable hand, should not be allowed to pass. After all opener should have no more than eight or nine tricks, and responder would only pass on a very weak hand. If opener is full value for ten tricks he should bid 2♥–2♠(Neg)–4♣/♦ to ensure hearing again from responder.

A positive response to an opening two bid is natural and shows a suit. Responder might have a problem hand as, for instance:

♠ Q 4   ♥ 9 6 3   ♦ A K 4   ♣ J 8 4 3 2

Over 2♠, with reasonable support for opener's suit, it is probably more useful to bid 3♦. But alter the hand to

♠ 9   ♥ Q J 4   ♦ A K 7 3   ♣ J 9 7 4 2

and opener can easily introduce a diamond suit. It only matters that partnerships agree on a policy that allows one to suggest a trump suit without the shackles of only bidding good suits.

The most useful positive bid is an immediate raise. This is unlimited, and as it agrees the trump suit, it assures opener that he is in the right strain. It will obviously guarantee the ability to make at least two tricks and, while most often responder will have an ace somewhere, this is by no means a necessity.

If for instance partner opened 2♥ and you held:

♠ K Q x   ♥ K J x   ♦ J x x   ♣ J x x x

it is really nonsense to consider any bid other than 3♥.

It has always been standard that a jump, from 2♥ to 4♥, should show a good trump support and no aces. This is still an efficient weapon, but it does consume a fair amount of space and it is self-defeating to have opener wondering just what kind of hand responder has if it can cover too many hand types. The bid must have definition, and thus while categorically denying holding an ace or a void, it should have good trump support and two outside second round controls. For instance:

♠ K 7		♠ K J 4 2	
♥ 10 6 4 2	or	♥ 9 8 7 3	
♦ K 9 3 2		♦ 5	
♣ Q 7 4		♣ Q J 8 7	

A response of 3NT over a two bid consumes much space, and should also be given some definition. It is fatuous to show just a balanced hand with a certain point count, because it is what kind of points and where they are that is of interest to the opener. So the jump to 3NT should show a balanced hand with about 11 points primarily made up of aces and kings. A hand that is largely composed of minor honours is extremely unlikely to lead to a slam unless opener takes violent action on the second round, and can be handled by making a negative response and then proceeding to game. If however the jump to 3NT guarantees three high cards, opener can proceed with some certainty on a slam hunt if that is what he needs.

It is a time-honoured principle that a jump response to a two bid shows a solid suit. Thus 2♥–3♠ shows a solid spade suit, such as:

A–K–Q–10–x–x–x   or   A–K–Q–J–x–x.

Very robust suits without solidarity can be dealt with naturally, i.e.:

2♥–2NT(spade Pos)–3♥–4♥

A jump to game in a new suit shows a long, one loser suit with no outside values, i.e. 2♥–4♠ would show a hand like:

♠ K Q J 10 9 x x   ♥ x x   ♦ x x   ♣ x x

This is yet another consistency in that we adopted the same procedure after an opening 2♣.

We all tend to accept certain treatments as normal without ever realising that in some situations they are superfluous. I am thinking of the 5NT Grand slam force which asks partner to bid a Grand slam if holding two of the top three honours in the agreed suit. After an opening two bid, the reasons for opener or responder to bid 5NT for this purpose are just about non-existent.

I suggest that having agreed a suit, either directly or by inference, a bid of 5NT should ask partner to bid the grand slam if the suit is solid in context. Suppose you held this hand:

♠ Q x x   ♥ x x   ♦ K Q J 10 x   ♣ A x x

What do you do when partner opens 2♥? You would respond a positive 3♦. If opener now rebids 3♥ one may logically wheel out Blackwood and should you hear the three ace response that you expect, it's now simply a matter of the solidarity of the hearts that concerns you. To ask for kings is relatively unimportant, and thus 5NT would ask opener to bid 7♥ if the suit was solid in context with the bidding. Had the bidding proceeded 2♥–3♦–4NT, by inference agreeing diamonds, and after your 5♦ response, opener bids 5NT, it would again be asking 'Are your trumps solid in context?' As partner has all the other three aces, they most certainly must be considered 'solid in context'.

Chapter 12.
Slam Bidding

After years of conducting bidding competitions, and discussing bidding with some of the world's best players, some conclusions can be reached. Whether the top bidders were Americans, Italians using their Roman, Neapolitan, Precision or Blue clubs, Israelis, Swedes or the brothers Sharples (the best natural bidders in the English style) there has always been a common denominator. All pairs that consistently have a great deal of accuracy at high level have rhythm and fluency. Irrespective of the method used, there was always a smoothness and an almost relaxed attitude in the conversation that is the easiest way to describe good bidding.

Artificial methods impose partnership restrictions because many bids have a systemic meaning. But the really good bidders are above the herd, because they use their highly developed judgement in deciding just what questions to ask and when to ask them; when to abandon their asking machinery and simply inform.

Many natural bidders transfer their allegiance to artificial systems, dissatisfied with their bidding. But much of any improvement is due to the fact that the partnership has got down to some study and practice for a change. Also some improvement may come from the fact that many areas of bidding are artificial, and so players can ask questions rather than think or use their judgement.

But ultimately, bad natural bidders become bad artificial bidders. If you could imagine Belladonna and Garozzo taking up Acol or the Sharples brothers taking up Precision, what would happen? The Italians would do well, because in addition to their magnificent judgement they would work on thousands of common situation to arrive at complete agreement. They would be bound to augment the system with hundreds of understandings and conventional aids etc.

The Sharples would learn all the system bids, until there was no danger of ever forgetting or misunderstanding. They would utilise the bids released by the new method such as 1♦—1♥—2NT. (2NT would not be natural.) They would amend, augment and evolve, and adapt tried and trusted treatments from their original methods. Both pairs would still be world class bidders. The basic ingredients for high accuracy would still be there, rhythm and an understanding of the necessity for hard work.

Let us try to isolate some of the aspects of big hand bidding that lead to a free flowing accurate exchange. Some have already been discussed with opening two bids, and others will be discussed in the chapter on conventional aids.

Some years ago when partnering Bob Sharples in a late round Gold Cup match I found myself in a dilemma. Bob's last bid was 5♦. We had agreed the heart suit and were sniffing at a slam. I felt, in general, that my hand was suitable but the only relevant card not so far shown to my partner was the spade king and this was worrying me. Eventually, bearing in mind that it is wrong to bid a slam unless you are sure that it is good proposition, I settled for 5♥.

When dummy was exposed Bob inquired what on earth I had found to think about. I explained my worry about the king of spades. His reply summarises what I would like to achieve in this chapter. He said: 'That is almost an insult to my bidding. Do you think that if the king of spades had been important I would not have so arranged the bidding that you could easily have shown that card?'

Look at the following bidding sequence, 1♥—2♥/3♠—4♣/4♦—4♥. How would you interpret the final bid of 4♥? Would you, as so many would, assume that this was just a continuation of the cue bid rhythm that had developed. If so, then I can assure you that your slam bidding is far from having the essential rhythm; and will certainly never have the accuracy necessary to reach the right target with a high degree of frequency. The argument is simple enough: it is rare that partner is going to be interested in hearing about a singleton or void in his own best suit. In fact it is rare that it is an asset; far more often it is worth a hole in the head. However, to hear of support for your suit, to know that the suit has been made more solid, to know that tricks are available is very often the key to the problem of discovering whether twelve tricks are available.

Cue bidding is obviously a better way of showing controls and investigating slams than the simple rustic use of Blackwood. However, most players tend to cue bid naively in mathematical fashion without any though for the relevance of the bids.

Take the following hand:

♠ A   ♥ A 10 9 8 7   ♦ A K 4 2   ♣ A 8 4

You open the bidding with 1♥ and partner replies with 3♥. I think we would all agree that the hand is worth two slam tries. Hands up all those who would now bid 3♠ in the normal style, cue bidding at what is apparently the most economical level. It is a stupid bid, and you can now take your hands down and feel grateful that you did not make the bid in front of a large audience. The correct bid is 4♣, knowing that almost certainly partner is going to sign-off in 4♥. After all, we do know that he is rather short in the ace department. Now we can cue bid 4♠ and already you can see the difference.

Your sequence would be 1♥–3♥/3♠–4♥/5♣ (maybe) and then what? Is partner to value the king of spades, is he to value spade holdings, is he able to show you the king of clubs that is so vital, is he to assume that you have both top honours in diamonds and good trumps? As it is, on the recommended sequence of 1♥–3♥/4♣–4♥/4♠, should partner have the king of clubs, a card that we know is so vital to the cause, he can economically show that card by bidding 5♣. No-one would really blame you for bidding 6♥ at this point but if you wish to be extra careful then you can now show the diamond control. The optimists amongst you would be looking at the possibilities of a grand slam if partner is holding just the right cards and intend to follow up by cue bidding diamonds twice.

The following suggestion may sound revolutionary to a lot of you and difficult to accept. But if you adopt a policy that a cue bid shows an ace, but the suit in which you cue is not necessarily the ace that you hold, and have partnership agreement about this, you won't come to any harm. Very often in high level sequences it is vital to show partner a singleton in an unbid suit because without this knowledge there can be no progress. If your partner then jumps to the slam on the basis of your supposed ace which in fact was a singleton, he will no doubt be compensated by the fact that you have an ace somewhere else.

I have known many players who after starting on an exchange of cue bids just continue cue bidding until they run out of bids, by which time they are at the slam level. All seem to overlook the basic truth of what cue bidding is all about. In essence the cue bid does not say to partner, as so many seem to take it, 'Partner will you bid the slam for me becuase I am too lazy?' It is more true to say that the cue bid denies the ability to bid the slam but announces the readiness to discuss the possibility.

Examine the following sequence, 1♥–3♥/4♣ –4♦/4♥–4♠/5♦. Now let us go through the thinking process and assume that the laws allow us to speak out loud rather than just make bids.

After 1♥–3♥ West says: 'Well, I know that your values are limited but bearing in mind that we have a heart fit there could well be a slam on. How do you feel about the idea? I do have a club control if that is any help.'

Responder then replies: 'As you say, I have limited my hand, but while still bearing in mind that limitation I am quite happy to discuss the prospect with you. Should it help you at all, I do have a control in diamonds.'

Notice that in no way has it been said that there is a slam on, just that they are prepared to discuss it. So we go on from there.

Opener would say: 'That's about it as far as I am concerned. I was prepared to have a brief discussion about the hand; we want to bid all these good slams, but I am not prepared to commit our side any further. I feel that I have said all there is to say about my hand unless you feel that you can proceed.'

4♠ now says: 'If you were prepared to make a slam try at all I am certainly sure that we are safe at the five level, I also have a spade control, a possible key factor, but I am still not prepared to bid the slam.'

5♦ would say: 'Thanks for the extra information and the continuing optimism, I also have a high card in diamonds that may or
may not be useful to the common cause but I'm afraid that I still
don't know enough to bid the slam. How do you feel about it?'

At this point East should be able to bid the slam or not with a
high degree of accuracy. The important point that I am trying to
get over is that slam bidding is a very relaxed and conversational
business. One expresses not just specific high cards via cue bids but
also a general picture of the possibilities and the conversation from
both sides of the table is measured in degrees of optimism and
pessimism rather than the location of one specific high card. By and
large, I think that players would get along quite well if they just
adopted a policy of saying to themselves: 'I like the hand' or 'I
don't like the hand'; just as simple as that. If partner makes a slam
try it means that facing a suitable hand a slam will be on, so if
your hand was suitable you could just bid the slam and if your
hand was unsuitable you could sign-off. Not very scientific I agree
BUT probably a lot more accurate in the end.

Suppose that you hold:

♠ A Q 4   ♥ A J   ♦ K Q J 10 5   ♣ A 4 2

You open a fairly obvious and automatic 2NT. Your partner
responds 3♠, a natural bid showing a spade suit. For all we know
he is just asking for our opinion as to the better game, 3NT or 4♠.
We are obviously going to select spades as the final spot but all
would agree that it costs nothing, on the way, to show our exceptional suitability. It could be that responder has the kind of hand
that is on the borders of the slam zone.

I imagine that most would bid 4♣ now, to agree spades and to
show the ace of clubs but if you look at the hand, this bid does
not make sense. Again in keeping with good slam bidding philoso-
phies, you need to tell partner things that are going to assist him in
judging whether or not a slam is on. Thus the right bid must be 4♦.

If partner assumes that you have the ace of diamonds and bids
6♠ do you really think that this can be a bad contract when he

knows nothing about the three aces that you hold? Of course, he may have adopted the policy that I suggested earlier and said: 'partner is interested in a slam and my hand looks good so therefore I will bid it because the slam try would not have been made without a hand of high suitability'. I just suggest to you that when a sequence starts 2NT–3 of a suit and you wish to agree that suit, it is better policy to tell responder where the tricks are going to come from, rather than tell him where one trick is going to come from. By bidding 4♣ you told him about one trick, by bidding 4♦ you told him that there were tricks available in that suit.

There are many semi-conventional gadgets that can be applied to bridge; a lot of them have been mentioned in this book. In talking of slam bidding, I would like you to examine the following hand

West	East
♠ A	♠ 10 8 4
♥ A K Q 10 8 7	♥ J 9 3
♦ 8 4	♦ A Q 3
♣ A K 10 3	♣ Q J 8 4

The bidding would normally be started, by West, with 2♥ and East would raise to 3♥, always the most constructive move after an opening two bid, to agree the opener's suit. Thereafter very few people would have any trouble in arriving at a slam. If you look at the hand 6♥ is undoubtedly solid, as is /NT. 7♥ depends on the diamond finesse, but 7♣ is a tremendously good contract and this is just the kind of hand that gains so many points in matches. As is so evident in the modern 'One club' systems, the first agreed suit tends to become the final contract. One of the assets of the natural bidding pair is that often they can find a second suit fit, that will provide more tricks; however it is not so easy after an opening two bid has been supported. At the table the bidding went 2♥–3♥ and at this point West decided that certainly 5♥ was safe enough facing a positive response and that some slam effort should be made. The bidding proceeded, West 2♥–3♥/5♣–5♠/5NT–7♣. All quite smooth. All quite simple. It just needed a partnership arrangement that after a suit has been agreed a jump in a new suit will guarantee at least four cards in the suit and they will be headed by the ace and king.

Raises of a major suit to the five level seem to cause some confusion. If a major suit has been agreed and then one partner or the other raises the major suit to the five level it is always, repeat always, a categoric demand that partner should bid the slam should he hold certain specific requirements.

If there is one unbid suit it would suggest that partner bid the slam if the unbid suit is controlled, furthermore, if holding the ace in the unbid suit partner has a duty to cue bid that suit. The knowledge that the suit is controlled completely is often enough information for the opener to bid a grand slam.

If there are two unbid suits and the major is raised to the five level, then the implication is very clear that both the unbid suits are controlled. After all is said and done, one is hardly likely to raise a major to the five level with two side suits wide open and if you were just interested in aces then the trusty Blackwood would serve the purpose. Thus this would be asking for trump quality.

On the following sequence, 1♠−3♠/4♣−4♦/5♠, the 5♠ bid demands that partner should bid six if the hearts are controlled and should partner hold the ace of hearts then he has a duty to bid 6♥ for the reasons afore stated. Now take another sequence, 1♠−3♠/4♣−4♦/4♥−4♠/5♠; all controls have been established thus 5♠ can only mean 'Partner, please bid the slam in spades if you think your trumps are good enough in context'. For those of you that use the Byzantine method of control asking which incorporates finding out about trump quality, these problems are frequently solved immediately.

Good players never bid a slam unless they know that the contract is going to be no worse than 50% when dummy hits the table. This means that the slam could well be lay-down, but at the worst will have a 50% chance. The corollary is that you should never bid a slam that you know to be at best a 50-50 chance before dummy does down. In fact it always ends by being worse than 50-50, and thousands more points are lost by bidding bad slams than by missing the occasional good one. As Reese commented in one of his books years ago 'You cannot bid them all, no pair can'.

There comes a time in every partnership when the lines of communication are obscured and no clear cut and concise path remains to exchange vital and accurate information. At this point it is better to write a slam off, than blunder on hopefully and wait with apprehension to see the dummy. A good bidder has seen the dummy before it goes down on the table. The Italians have also taught us a great deal about another aspect of slam bidding, that while never bidding slams on hope or speculation, one must never be too lazy to use the machinery which exists.

When discussing bridge with America's biggest master point winner, T.V. producer Barry Crane, he said that he made a point never to play an 'if' game. When I asked him to elucidate he said that as soon as you find yourself saying 'If my partner has five diamonds' or 'If my partner has five spades to the jack' or if this or if that, then forget it; only the losers play the 'if' game. Of course he agreed that sometimes you can find out if partner has the vital cards or distributional assets, and it is just plain laziness not to do so; but if you can't find out, don't hope, don't play the 'if' game.

BYZANTINE BLACKWOOD

This control asking method, brain child of Jack Marx, was christened in logical fashion. After Blackwood we had Roman Blackwood and after the Roman empire came Byzantine. The logic continues through the treatment. It parallels other control asking methods in that 4NT is the enquiry vehicle and also in that a trump agreement must exist, either by direct or implied support.

I normally leave technique until the end and concentrate on the philosophy, but in this case it is probably easier to follow usual procedure. However, don't skip the commentary on the thinking that follows later.

4NT asks: then **5♣** = 0 or 3 aces. There are assumed to be five aces, the trump king counting as the extra one.

5♦ = 1 or 4 aces, again with five ace availability.

$5\heartsuit$ = 2 aces or one ace plus KQ of trumps. NOTE: One ace plus the trump king does not qualify. You must have two aces. A third possibility is one ace plus two kings in agreed suits. Some players also add one ace plus the trump king plus any king of a suit bid naturally by the 4NT bidder.

$5\spadesuit$ = 2 aces plus KQ of trumps, or 2 aces plus kings in two agreed suits. Again, you might include 2 aces plus the trump king plus a king of a naturally bid suit by the enquirer.

5NT= 3 aces plus KQ of trumps, or 4 aces plus the trump king, or 2 aces plus KQ of trumps plus a king of a second agreed suit.

If you are thinking on the right lines, you will see that the object is to locate key cards. Many find it difficult to memorise this list, but it is fairly simple if you remember that $5\clubsuit/5\diamondsuit$ are in accordance with the familiar Roman Blackwood. $5\heartsuit$ shows either two aces or three key cards, $5\spadesuit$ shows four key cards and 5NT shows five key cards. Don't forget that a $5\spadesuit$ (four key card) response, cannot be three aces plus the trump king. That holding is shown as four aces via $5\diamondsuit$.

One must stick to the principles of all control asking in that the answer to the question should solve your problem. Thus, as in Blackwood, one never asks via 4NT with two losers in an unbid suit. Neither does it work if you have a void. This apart, you will find that adopting Byzantine will lead to a much greater frequency of asking, as the reply gives so much more information.

Responder is permitted to jump to the six level with a working void but — the hand must include two aces or one ace and the KQ of trumps, in other words a $5\heartsuit$ response. If responder had three aces, or any holding not mentioned above, the simple response must be used ignoring the void. There are sometimes areas of doubt when the response is $5\clubsuit$ or $5\diamondsuit$. It is possible to construct hands when the lower holding exists. Thus, however certain the 4NT bidder is about the response, he MUST assume the lower and responder MUST bid on with the higher. In fact, this can lead to added useful information being transmitted. For example, assuming an agreed spade suit and a response of 5♣ to a 4NT enquiry, there will be an automatic sign off in 5♠, but holding the three aces, the 5♣ bidder will proceed. He may be able to bid 5NT/6♣/6♦/6♥ with some highly suitable hand to show a hitherto unspecified high card.

There is a genuine problem when you have agreed a minor suit and the response to 4NT is five of the agreed minor. Whilst the asker will usually know what the responder holds, if it is impossible for you to have a 5NT reply (in other words, you cannot have enough strength), you should bid 5NT to clarify the situation for partner. For instance, if after opening a weak no trump, you get around to agreeing clubs and at some stage partner enquires via 4NT and you hold two aces plus the club king, reply 5NT to eliminate doubt.

If after going through the 4NT process, one then tries 5NT, this is again an enquiry. It asks if responder has any undisclosed tricks. The answers are parallel to the lower range of replies to 4NT, i.e. 5♣ would show 0 or 3 extra tricks, 5♦ 1 or 4 extra tricks, 5♥, 2 extra tricks. Obviously any undisclosed king would count as an extra trick, but one also includes KQ in the same suit as two tricks. The trump queen can also be regarded as an extra trick. Remember, responder only shows high cards that have not already been included in the response to 4NT.

One important factor is that the trump queen must not be shown as one extra trick if it is the only undisclosed high card; it can only be included in conjunction with some other value, such as a side suit king. It is usual for the opener to ask for the trump queen via the Baron grand slam try; that means bidding six of the suit below the agreed suit, thus a 5NT enquiry is only used when other vital information is required.

You will find that apart from — as mentioned — the greater frequency that will come, Byzantine has particular value in investigating grand slams. Another of its major advantages is that often you will be able to write off the slam because you will know that two key cards are missing. As in employing any convention, it is important to try to understand the underlying philosophy and not just memorise a series of questions and answers. It would be simple enough to quote masses of examples, but a little thought will soon lead you into so gearing the bidding so that the right hand is in the position to use Byzantine — the hand that will obtain the greater useful information. You will soon register the negative inferences that abound. If, for example, my partner exbarks on a slam hunting route that does not include 4NT, then it is clear that specific information is being sought, that could not be obtained by the conventional enquiry. If after hearing a reply to 4NT, partner explores a grand slam without using the 5NT bid, he is again requesting specific information. Often we reach a position when we know that all the key cards are in the required place but that the grand slam will depend on partner holding a particular king. The message will be loud and clear if we make our grand slam try by bidding the suit, rather than asking the 5NT question that will tell us of an extra king but not specify the precise card.

In some cases, a bid is made that specifically agrees a suit and guarantees first round control such as 1♥—1♠—4♣/4♦. As this can be either ace or void it MUST be left out of any answer to 4NT.

Partnerships will need to discuss these matters and it will help to bid a lot of big hands to develop a feeling of comfort. Just remove some of the low cards and ensure that nearly every hand is in the slam zone. No doubt, players will provide their own 'improvements', but remember that there may be hidden traps that were considered by those who developed the method so stick with the suggested treatment to start with. Of course, you will find for yourselves facts that have not been included; for instance, an opening 1NT bidder (12-14), can never be in a position to bid 4NT as asking.

Chapter 13.
Competitive Bidding

Defensive bidding is based on concepts that are not similar to those we have considered in uncontested auctions. Left to our own devices, the aim is to have a conversation giving the fullest possible exchange of information, before deciding on the final resting spot.

But when your opponents have opened the bidding, your side is, theorectically, on the defensive, no matter how strong you are. There is always the danger that responder can raise the opening bid to some high level, and it is thus naive to hope that you can have an uncluttered sequence in competition. Our thinking should, consequently, be along assertive rather than interrogative lines. To start with a simple overcall, this can no longer be regarded as the start of a conversation, but much more as a statement of fact.

Time has not changed the old Culbertson rule of 'two and three', which says that all defensive bids should guarantee sufficient tricks in play to ensure that the loss should be no more than two down when vulnerable or three down when not vulnerable. This is the price we are prepared to pay for preventing the opponents making game. But there is a most important, and overlooked, point. While we are prepared to risk minus 500 to save an enemy game, we should not be prepared to lose anything to save the opponents from disaster, or from reaching a contract that could not possibly succeed. Thus, the defensive values shown by an overcall etc. should be strictly limited, especially when one has the dilemma of whether or not to bid.

Every bid at bridge is made for the reason that you expect to gain more than you lose. For instance, you may open 1♥ with the following hand:

♠ A 8 3   ♥ A 7 5 3 2   ♦ K 8 4   ♣ K 2

It could be that left hand opponent doubles and right hand opponent passes, and you are left to play in 1♥, doubled ending with a penalty in four figures. But this will not stop you opening the next time you get dealt a similar hand, because you know that you stand to gain much more by opening on 14 point hands than by passing.

In defensive bidding it is a little more difficult to assess the pros and cons because no mathematical guidelines can be laid down. It is fair enough to say that if you overcall an opening 1♥ bid with 2♦ you should make at least the requisite 5 or 6 tricks. But suppose you held:

♠ K 10 3   ♥ K J 7   ♦ A K 9 7 3   ♣ 7 5

While it is true that if you are doubled you can reasonably expect to lose no more than 500 points, what is the chance that the enemy can make a sound game? It is not a fair swap to lose 500 points against what is, at best, a part score from your opposition.

Of course there are tactical considerations. If the opening bid is 1♦, for example, and you overcall 1♥, left hand opponent can make any bid that he may have intended to make without your intervention. 1♥/1NT/2♣/2♦ are all available to him, and since you have done nothing to disrupt the free flow of information between your opponents, you can only hope to gain by having a reasonable chance of outbidding the enemy and buying the contract.

If, however, there is an opening bid of 1♣ and you overcall 1♠, despite the increasing use of negative (Sputnik) doubles, left hand opponent can no longer bid so easily. You will have caused considerable difficulty for the opposition in their exchange of information. This advantage is increased on those occasions that your partner can raise your overcall, creating an even more pre-emptive effect.

Those who employ negative doubles will claim that the 1♠ intervention does no particular harm, but if you consider the following hand after the bidding has gone 1♣ –1♠, you will see that all is not easy for your opponents. Also on those occasions when your overcall proves to have been made at a badly chosen moment, the penalty double is no longer available to the enemy.

♠ 10 6 4   ♥ A 8 3   ♦ K Q 9 5   ♣ J 7 4

When using negative doubles, left hand opponent is often forced to pass for want of a better bid with fair values, but without four hearts. Thus opener is expected to reopen on less values than he would some years ago. Again we have a problem arising for the opponents. How does responder know whether opener has reopened with plus values, or with suitable minimum values, and on what basis does he bid? If he bids on the basis of his partner being minimum then it means that opener must make a further move if his reopening was more robust. Already we can see that the auction might be getting uncomfortably amorphous, and we have not yet considered the opportunities for the partner of the overcaller to wait for you to reach a level at which he can double. So an ordinary hand that, 30 years ago, would have been dealt with without too much trouble, suddenly becomes a modern day disaster.

The response to an overcall is another area of bidding given little thought. Again, we probably muddle along with only the occasional calamity that we can erase so easily from memory.

A simple raise must change in emphasis depending on the auction. (a) 1♦—1♠—Pass 2♠ and (b) 1♦—1♠—2♥—2♠ are very different. In case (a) the opponents have not yet got together, so much is gained by raising the ante to make it difficult without serious risk. In case (b) a fair amount of information has already been exchanged so the raise to 2♠ can only sensibly mean that there is a realistic hope of outbidding them.

A change of suit should be assumed to be neutral and in no way encouraging. Having said this, bearing in mind that we trust the original overcall to be sound in trick taking potential, there is no great premium on 'rescuing'. The original overcaller should bid on with plus values, particularly with some fit.

A no-trump bid facing an overcall is bound by the logic that governs all no trump bidding. A simple beginner's table would read: 'I need 21/22 points to make seven tricks — 23/24 to make eight and 25/26 to make nine'. Of course one takes into account the tricks promised, but as an overcall does not show the high card points necessary to open the bidding, a no trump response should be a little stronger than to an opening bid.

Sometimes one must insist on partner bidding again — even after a simple overcall. You can jump in a new suit if it seems best or bid the enemy suit — the ubiquitous cue bid, much maligned because of its constant misuse. A good general rule is to regard the bid of the enemy suit as forcing to suit agreement — a rebid suit to be regarded as agreed. Thus:

1♥	1♠	Pass 2♥		1♥	1♠	Pass 2♥
Pass 2♠ is non-forcing				Pass 1♠	Pass 3♣ is forcing	

Certainly competitive bidding is the area in which most partnerships have problems of definition. One of the most valuable bids — that I consider to be grossly underused — is Pass. When we open the bidding with one of a suit we undertake to make a rebid if responder makes an unlimited bid, thus keeping open the lines of communication. But should the bidding proceed 1♠ by you — Pass — 2♣ — 2♦ it is obvious enough that you are not needed to keep the bidding open. This is what I meant when I said that the Pass is undervalued. Far too many players would rebid 2♠ just because they would have bid 2♠ had the matter been forced upon them. To pass at this stage is to transmit a very clear message.

Partner also knows that under other circumstances you would have had a duty to keep the bidding open and thus by passing you are saying as clearly as if you were holding your cards the other way around, that your opening bid was minimum and any further venture must be up to your partner. He cannot expect any more from you than that which he already knows, i.e. a spade suit and a minimum opening bid. He can draw other inferences by simply asking himself what were you intending to rebid had your opponent not accommodatingly entered the fray to give you this extra means of communication.

It naturally follows that should you bid, you are showing extra values; there is one exception to this and that is when you show support. I think that the idea that support shows extra values became extinct before the Dodo. Had you intended to support your partner without the intervention, then there is no logical reason why you should not support after the intervention without showing extra values. After all is said and done, you do have the values to make the contract that you have just suggested.

This apart, assume the bidding starts as before, 1♠ — Pass — 2♣ —2♦ —? and at this point you choose to bid 2♥; apart from simply saying that you have hearts as well as spades, the hand should also be a little more robust than just some very minimum opener, because if your side has the wherewithal to outbid the opponents, it is for sure that your partner will continue the bidding. The same could be said about a voluntary rebid of 2♠. When you open the bidding with 1♠ we all know that with 12 or 13 high card points and a five card suit we would open. The opponent's intervention has now meant that you can rebid 2♠ with some plus values. It could be that the plus value could be in terms of suit quality or length or slight additional values, as for instance a good six card suit and 12 or 13 high card points etc. etc.

Another rarely discussed situation between partners is when the sequence goes as follows, with you sitting in the South seat,

West	North	East	South
—	1♠	Pass	Pass
1NT	Pass	Pass	Dble

Just what should this mean?

There are two schools of thought on this point; it can be suggested that the double should now say that you have support for clubs, diamonds and hearts and thus partner can bid any of these suits in comfort. However, experience has shown that, apart from the rarity of the hand type, all too often the poor opener is left with no action available to him other than to rebid his own suit, the suit that you have shown an active dislike for. Or he can always pass 1NT doubled and let them make a plus score much in excess of their expectations. The second, more intelligent use of the bid is to say: 'I would have raised you to 2♠ having already limited my hand quite severely by passing your opening bid. But why should I raise you to 2♠ when you can do this for yourself?' Meanwhile you may have been dealt with a very high point count and it may well be that the opponents have chosen a very unfortunate moment to enter the arena. The ideal hand of this type would be one similar to the following which occured in tournament play:

♠ J 6 4   ♥ J 10 8 6   ♦ Q 10 7 3   ♣ 6 5

The vulnerability was game all and the bidding went as mentioned. With this hand South doubled 1NT, bearing in mind the partnership arrangement that it was in effect a raise to 2♠; opener, with 18 points and knowing of some spade support opposite, was able to pass and collect 500 points, as against the 110 that would have been collected had the side played in 2♠, as happened in the other room.

A fairly parallel situation occurs when left hand opponent opens the bidding, partner passes, the hand on the right bids 1NT, limited; what would a double by you mean now? In time honoured fashion it tended to show a powerful hand in keeping with most doubles of 1NT; i.e. business. It does not take much examination for one to realise that the frequency of this type of hand and that where you would like your partner to bid something bear no comparison. Thus it is suggested that should the bidding so 1♠—Pass—1NT—Dble that this should be taken as a take-out double of 1♠. In the chapter on conventions which deals more fully with competitive doubles you will see the tremendous degree of flexibility that is available to partnerships by the adoption of this general method.

Another general recommendation that I would make that often leads to good results is to adopt an overall policy that in competitive auctions, a double of a suit naturally bid on your left should be regarded as competitive, i.e. a hand that is in general suitable for defence, but partner is allowed to exercise his option to remove it. Whereas, a double of a suit on your right should be strictly for business. This type of situation most frequently occurs after an opening bid of 1NT by the opponents, especially when it is a weak no-trump. Take as an example the following sequence:

West	North	East	South
1NT	Dble	2♣	Pass
Pass	?		

Nowadays most players would agree that the situation is forcing. Some would go so far as to say that whenever the opponents have been doubled in 1NT and rescued themselves, all passes should be forcing on the basis that they have announced that they do not have the ability to make 1NT. This is carrying things just a little too far and readily lends itself to opponents having an axe hanging over your head. Playing against a world class pair who adopt this system, that all passes are forcing, in this situation, I once had the great pleasure of rescuing my partner from 1NT doubled with a 5—4—3—1, 10 point hand knowing that the opponents would be forced to either bid or double; the choice that was left to them was that either we played in 2♥ doubled which would have made with one overtrick or they played in 2NT, as they did, for a penalty of 1400.

When responder removes to two of a minor it is often the start of a rescue operation and apart from that there is a element of safety in that there is a likelihood that your side can bid at the two level. If the opponents rescue into two of a major e.g. 1NT—Dble—2♥—Pass—Pass—? it is not so clear cut and certainly the rescuer is unlikely to be playing jokes. So we have a general principle that a rescue of two of a minor passed back to the doubler, will create a forcing situation. A rescue of two of a major passed back to the original doubler would create a situation in which both partners would know that every effort would be made to keep the bidding open, but one is allowed to exercise an option to pass.

Having gone this far, it follows automatically that should the bidding proceed 1NT—Dble—2♣ —2♥, then obviously the person who bid 2♥ is weak. With a five card heart suit and some reasonable values, six points or so, he could always pass knowing that you are forced to bid, and then bid hearts showing the moderate values. It would still apply had the bidding proceeded 1NT—Dble—2♣ —3♥. The person who bid 3♥ has announced no defensive values.

To get back to the point from which we have rather digressed. Should the bidding proceed 1NT—Dble—2♥—Pass—Pass—Dble, the suggestion is that the bid should just show a hand that is suitable for defence, but partner may exercise his option to remove the double for reasons of unsuitability or safety. One can often pick up good penalties by adopting this procedure.

As I have said, the most frequent time that this situation is going to arise is after 1NT has been doubled, but let us take a parallel situation. At game all you hold:

♠ K 9 6   ♥ A 10 5   ♦ A J 8 6   ♣ K 7 4

and as dealer, playing weak no-trump, you open the bidding with 1♦. Your left hand opponent doubles and your partner redoubles. After the pass on your right, in time honoured style you pass showing a good hand and hear 1♠ on your left. It is accepted that, at this point, should partner double 1♠ this would be for business, but suppose instead he passed the ball back to you. Thus you have the problem of what to do. The common view was to make the natural rebid of 1NT, which would show in partnership style 15-16 points. However, adopting our suggested principles, you can double 1♠ simply to show a hand that is in general good for defence and of neccessity this would suggest a hand that is relatively balanced. When the hand occured the suggested double was passed out, partner holding Q–10–5 of spades amongst his balanced 10 points and a penalty of 800 was collected when game was, to say the least, only a probability.

Having introduced the redouble into the chapter, it would seem a good idea to discuss this whole area. After an opening bid has been doubled by left hand opponent it has always been accepted that a redouble would show a hand that had its sights set on future axe wielding or a hand that was too strong to express itself in some other way. There is a growing school of thought that one should ignore the take-out double and bid quite naturally, thus 1♥– Dble–1♠ would be a forcing bid of unlimited value in much the same way as it would have been without the intervening double. However I am content with the more relaxed style with which I am familiar, in that a bid after a double should be regarded as neutral. Obviously there will be times when one would bid a new suit as a simple rescue operation for fear that the take-out double will be converted for penalties, as for instance should you hold:

♠ Q 10 9 7 6 5   ♥ 2   ♦ 10 9 4   ♣ 8 6 3

and partner's opening bid of 1♥ is doubled; it seems right to bid 1♠ in case left hand opponent choses to pass 1♥ doubled, an occurrence that would leave you feeling rather uncomfortable. However, should you hold:

♠ A J 10 9 6   ♥ Q J 3   ♦ J 6 4   ♣ 6 5

and the bidding proceeded the same way, 1♥ from partner and a double on the right, it is so sensible to show the spade suit while the opportunity exists. Thus it becomes encumbent upon the opener to make a rebid in fairly natural style whilst bearing in mind the possibility that your bid was made in fear and trembling, rather than for more constructive purposes.

Many hands do lend themselves to the redouble as the best way of collecting possible penalties or subsequently establishing a forcing conversation between the two partners that is so essential to good bidding. A sequence such as

1♥   Dble   Rdble   Pass
1♠

would be regarded as natural and eschewing any penalty. A sequence such as

1♥   Dble   Rdble   Pass
Pass 1♠   2♣

would be regarded as not only natural, but also as forcing and a complete parallel with the situation 1♥–Pass–2♣. It is technically, and in practice, efficient that having redoubled, the opening bidder should not bid in front of you in a competitive auction for the reason stated. Your intention may be to punish the opponents. Thus it would follow that the sequence

1♥–Dble–Rdble–1♠
2♥

should show a weak opening bid. It is not wise to bid 2♥ with a reasonable opening bid, just because one thinks that you are not going to be prepared to pass any business double. You can always pass the action round to the redoubler and then, should he double for business, remove the double to 2♥, or anything else and the message passed is very clear, that whilst in now way being short of an opening bid, your hand is in no way suitable for the defensive suggestion made by your partner.

Following this through to its logical conclusion, it would mean to bid in front of the redoubler shows a hand of less than the expected strength. This would just as equally apply should the bid be a jump as in the sequence

1♥   Dble   Rdble   1♠
3♦

The opener should have something like:

♠ 6   ♥ K Q 10 9 8 6   ♦ A J 10 9 8   ♣ 4

or a hand of similar type. In an international match, not so long ago, on an identical sequence,

1♥   Dble   Rdble   Pass
3♦   Pass?

the original redoubler held:

♠ A 6 4   ♥ A 3   ♦ A 5 4 2   ♣ 8 6 4 2

and had no trouble in bidding 6♦, a contract that was completely solid facing a 10 point opening bid and was not even dreamt of in the other room.

In the hurly burly of the present day game the accent is more and more on aggression as more and more pairs realise that to put pressure on the opponents is to the ultimate good of your side. Thus, in competition, one tends to bid more aggressively than was normal in the past; this particularly applies in the area that can be generally called 'Protection'. It is now almost impossible, in the tournament world, to get away with such a sequence as 1♥–Pass–2♥–Pass–Pass–Pass. It seems almost inevitable that the person in the last seat will reopen the bidding. At the same time the protection can be so ill-advised as to suggest that the defending side need protection from each other. There was a recent case where the sequence 1♥—Pass—1♠—Pass/2♥—Pass—2♠—Pass/Pass— was now continued by an intervention of 2NT requesting partner to choose a minor. Partner who had a doubleton in each minor was left with the choice of making the right guess to lose 800 or the wrong guess to lose 1100.

The reason that the protection was so unwise is mathematically very easy to explain. Ask yourself this question: 'Should the opponents have nine cards in a suit between them (a likelihood should the bidding proceed something like 1♦—Pass—2♦), what are the chances of us having a genuine 4—4 fit in a suit of our own?' It isn't difficult to work it out but take my word for it; in fact it is a stone cold certainty that if they have a suit with nine cards between them then you must have a suit with at least eight cards between your two hands. Even when the opponents only hold an eight card trump fit the odds are extremely high that you also have an eight card fit available. Thus just as one makes a take-out double of an opening bid with fairly light values, 12 or 13 points, and with the ideal distribution, i.e. genuine support for the unbid suits because of the safety element involved, in that your side should find some satisfactory resting spot, it becomes even more sure that your side will find some genuine fit in sequences where your opponents have voluntarily shown that they have a mutually agreeable suit.

The theory can be carried to ridiculous extremes. Supposing that the bidding went

1♦   Pass 2♦   Pass—
Pass?

back to you. Carry on with our fantasy that so far you have not yet picked up your hand and when you do so, you find that you have some kind of one point, relatively balanced hand. If we assume that the opponents' bidding is sound; that the opening bidder has an opening one bid and not an opening two bid and is not strong enough to make a game try facing a limited response, and that the responder has in fact the weak hand promised by the bidding, it is mathematically obvious that your side has as much right to play the hand as theirs in overall values. Furthermore, as explained, it is almost certain that your side will have some mutually agreeable trump suit.

Quite obviously the situation is absurd unless of course your partner has accidentally fallen asleep or passed by accident with the 19 or 20 points that he must hold.

In protective situations, partners should consider how best to show the hand type with which they are trying to create the extra problem for the opponents by raising the ante a little. Let's take, as a base for discussion, the sequence 1♥—Pass—2♥—Pass—Pass—? Obviously, if you hold support for all three suits other than hearts, the take-out double suggests itself immediately. If your suits include spades and diamonds, again a take-out double suggests itself as the most efficient action, always bearing in mind that we are basing the bidding on the valid assumption that our side will have a mutually agreeable trump suit somewhere. Should your partner bid clubs, an idea that does not appeal to you, you can then bid diamonds and partner will know that your hand includes diamonds and spades and then the fit will be found. One can bid 2NT, obviously not a natural bid, and thus show both minor suits. It logically follows that if you bid 2♠ — taking into account the normal aggressive tactics of the modern day player who would overcall 1♠ on a few high cards and a sprig of four leafed clover — what would it mean at this point? It can only suggest that your suits are spades and possibly clubs.

One very important aspect for partners to agree in this situation is that just as it aids your competitive efficiency to be busy commensurate with common sense and safety, the object of the exercise is going to be self defeating if both players keep bidding. In our quoted example, 1♥—Pass—2♥—Pass—Pass—, should you now protect in some form or another and your partner þid a contract that meets with your approval and the opponents then bid 3♥, only under the most exceptional circumstances should either of you proceed further.

It is a simple enough proposition to understand and accept; for my part I would sooner defend against 3♥ than 2♥ and if very occasionally we miss a game then I am prepared to accept this as a small price to pay for the frequency with which I am able to get back into the bidding in the balancing seat. Sometimes one is wrong to protect in the first place in that the opponents were due to fail by one in their contract and you are going to fail by one in your contract, but by and large you will find that as often as you are wrong, they will make you right by bidding one more anyway.

Chapter 14.

Conventions and Conventional Aids

A conventional bid is one which sounds natural but isn't. It is a cypher. Since the earliest days of bridge, players have invented codified uses for bids and undoubtedly the process will go on *ad infinitum*.

Whenever we choose to discard a natural bid in favour of a conventional understanding we lose the natural bid, and must carefully review the pros and cons. One of the first considerations is how useful is the natural bid, and how much will we gain by the introduction of an artificial meaning? What is the frequency of the new, magnificent addition to our vocabulary? And — what is the frequency of gain when the new weapon is brought into use?

Never let us forget that when we give an artificial meaning to a bid, we automatically impose an extra strain on the fallibility of the human memory. Such is the injustice of bridge that bad bidding and less than perfect approaches often lead to satisfactory results. It is easy, but of little gain, to complain that your new wonder bid got you to the perfect spot for all the right reasons, while the other idiots got there via a 'it looks about right' approach. But — just one misunderstanding, one mis-interpretation and it would have been better to have remained with your bow and arrow.

If you manage to arrive scientifically in six clubs on a two-one fit, it does not take a mathematical genius to work out that you need about five successes to get back to even. I am not knocking progress. At heart I know that I am a scientist and want to improve my vocabulary, even if the gain is minimal, but I am also a realist. One could invent an opening bid of 5♦ to show:

♠ A K x x x   ♥ A K x x x   ♦ —   ♣ x

and it is obvious that it would be of inestimable value when the hand occurred. Meanwhile, we would have to wait many years for it to crop up; and when it did, despite the beauty of our method, we would probably chicken out because we would not be certain that the ox opposite would remember.

By all yardsticks a Stayman 2♣ bid over an opening 1NT is an advance. We lose only a paltry 2♣ contract, and that often is not the only good spot. We gain in many ways and the frequency of gain is heavily weighted in our favour. We get enough practice for the bid to become second nature.

In many parts of this book, treatments are recommended that can only be used by partnership agreement. The following conventions blend in with our bidding philosophy; they have all been tried and tested, and all have high frequency of gain. Take them or not, but if you do, make sure that the ideas are fully understood and agreed. If you are not prepared to do the work necessary to make conventional aids a comfort, a fluent part of your vocabulary, then stick to bidding by the seat of your pants. It is no coincidence that when two good players get together for the first time they inevitably do well. They haven't had time to develop 'expert' misunderstandings.

(a) Transfers over 1NT

The economy and gain in communication of transfer bids are immense. There are a number of different, detailed systems, but whichever one you adopt, it should apply whenever the first natural bid by your side is 1NT: (a) an opening 1NT. (b) an over-call of 1NT, whether immediate or protective. (c) in strong club systems when the bidding starts 1♣ —1 any—1NT.

There are many good methods on the market, and we suggest you take one, rather than do the work all over again. The follow-ing is our style, and it has worked well for 15 years with many gains. The general plan is to keep memory strain to a minimum, and to concentrate on accuracy at the game and higher levels, where there is more chance of big gains and losses.

1NT—3 suit. This is natural and shows genuine slam potential Opener is expected to bid any suit below 3NT without promising extra values, in case responder is two suited. A simple raise shows a minimum, but a four level bid agrees responder's suit and is a cue bid. Advantages? You both know of the slam ambition, and so conduct the conversation with this in mind. However strong the responder sounds in other sequences, he was not worth an immediate slam try.

1NT—2NT. Interested in a slam with a balanced hand. The bid is 'Baron', and suits should next be bid in ascending order, because a 4—4 fit could be the key Should opener choose to bid 3NT over 2NT, the message is 'drop dead', and if responder then bids on, he's good.

1NT- 2♣. Stayman, per se. Opener bids 2♦ with no major, 2♥ with hearts or both majors and responder must be careful to bid 2♠ with a four card suit. Do not forget that this is the only way to make a quantitative raise to 2NT. If after opener's reply, responder bids 3♣/3♦, this is natural, forcing and is likely to be a probe for the best contract. All bidding is common-sense, and forcing to four of the minor.

1NT—2♣ —2♦—3♥. Non-forcing. Five-five in the majors. If opener shows a major after two clubs pot game.

1NT—2♣—2♦—3♥.   Forcing, with five-five in the majors. If opener bids a major, follow it through in case a slam is on with a super fit. 1NT—2♣—2♥—3♠ or 1NT—2♣—2♠—3♥ would still be game forcing with 5—5 in the majors.

1NT—2♦/2♥.   Shows at least five of the next suit up. Opener will normally do just as requested and transfer. With an EXCEPTIONAL fit and good controls, opener can break the transfer and show his bad suit — similar in style to a normal trial bid. 1NT—2♦—2♠ would show a super fit for hearts, and help needed in spades. Responder's bid of a second suit is natural and forcing. If opener gives simple preference or a simple raise, responder may next pass. If after the transfer, responder raises i.e. 1NT—2♦—2♥—3♥, he is making a game try with a not very good suit. If after the transfer, responder jumps in a second suit, this shows two GOOD suits and nothing outside.

1NT—2♦—2♥—4♣   = ♠x x ♥A K J 10 8 ♦x ♣A K Q x x. (Remember, with more we would start 1NT—3♥).

1NT—2♠.   Compulsory transfer to 2NT. If responder then bids three of any suit, he is making a non-forcing game try with a good suit. Note the difference bewteen 1NT—2♠—2NT—3♥ and 1NT—2♦—2♥—3♥.

If after 2NT responder bids at the four level, 4♣/♦ shows a slam try with 5—3—3—2 and a 5 card minor. There is an inference that the suit is not great or we might have bid 1NT—3♣/3♦ direct. 4♥ = 4—3—3—3 with a top honour in each suit, minimum slam try. 4♠ is a parallel, with a maximum slam try. 4NT is a simple quantative raise to 4NT, without a five card suit, an ace or king in each suit or particular interest in finding a four—four fit.

You will see that after a response of 2♠, you only have to remember that the next bid is either a 'good suit' game try or a balanced hand slam try. If you forget the exact meaning, you will at least be in a sensible sort of contract. The rest is exotica.

1NT 4NT.   A big (not enough for a genuine slam try) minor two suiter with no major suit control (6—5—1—1). With a similar hand with a first round control outside, bid the control and then leap to 5♣. INT—2♥—2♠—5♣ would be a minor 6—5 with first round heart control. Even if you have to wait a while, it will be worth it to see the opponents' faces when the bidding goes 1NT—2♥—2♠—5♣—7♦.

I make no claim that this system is ideal, but I know that it works well on the hands that matter.

(b) Baron 2NT

The primary object of the Baron 2NT response to an opening bid of one of a suit is to deal with the otherwise awkward strong, balanced hand. All too often the bid is mis-used, almost abused, and it is wrong to use the convention indiscriminately rather than go to the trouble of thinking out a more accurate, simple approach. Used correctly, the bid is a great help, not only to describe a difficult hand, but also to differentiate it from other hands. After a suit opening, a response of 2NT should show:-

(a) A balanced hand with 16—19 points.
(b) No good five card suit. For clarity a good suit could be defined as two of the top three, or three of the top five honours.
(c) All unbid suits guarded.

After 2NT, opener should proceed to bid naturally and descriptively. A simple raise to 3NT should show a minimum hand with no ambition. A bid of 4NT by either hand should be assumed to be natural. Opener would show any second suit if biddable or rebid his suit if he felt that this was the most useful information. A reverse, whilst not needing full strength, should have plus values.

The most essential part of the convention is that an accurate limitation is established at an early stage. Without this, partners are always in doubt as to whether encouraging bids are made with plus values, or because minimum hands are regarded as highly suitable. After opener's rebid, responder must define his range. After 1♥—2NT—3♣, a simple preference to 3♥, a simple raise to 4♣, or a rebid of 3NT all show a minimum 16/17 points. Jump preference, or a new suit (3♦/3♠/4♥) would show that responder held 18/19 points. Some players add that a jump to 4NT would show 20/21 balanced points, extending the usefulness of the convention.

It is probably helpful to show a couple of bad results that came from a mis-use of the system:

```
♠ K 6 4              ♠ A J 10
♥ K Q 10 7 5 2       ♥ A J 4
♦ 5                  ♦ J 8 3
♣ K 5 4              ♣ A Q 8 3
```

West	East
1♥	2NT
3♥	4♥
Pass	

Opener thought that there would be too many gaps to fill to make a slam a good proposition. East was likely to hold wasted diamond values. Instead, had the bidding gone 1♥–3♣–3♥–4♥, there would have been no problem for West, he could simply wheel out 4NT.

```
♠ K 10 7             ♠ Q 7 4
♥ A Q 8 4 2          ♥ K 6
♦ A 4                ♦ K 9 7 3
♣ J 9 5              ♣ A K Q 10
```

West	East
1♥	2NT
3♥	3NT
4NT	6NT

The East hand is eminently suitable for a minor suit slam. In a sense, East was lucky that partner bid on after his calculated underbid of 3NT. When the hand occurred, the other pair did not play Baron 2NT, and the bidding was 1♥–3♣–3♥–3NT–4♣–4♦–6♣.

The Baron 2NT bid is designed to ease the way when the difficult hands arrive, but like many other conventions it should not be used as a substitute for thinking.

(c) Negative (or Sputnik) Doubles

I lay no claim to be expert in using negative, (or Sputnik) doubles. Probably it is because I don't like the general principle. Apart from the fact that I seem to get along well enough without them, I have seen too many monstrosities perpetrated in the name of Sputnik. Even if bad results come about mostly because of mistakes, I still do not like gadgets that lead players into troubled waters. But since many great players do use negative doubles, they must be examined.

In its basic form, the negative double is used after an opening bid and an intervention. The principle is that responder to an opening bid finds that the enemy intervention has produced a bidding problem that can be solved by doubling — for take-out. This loses the immediate business double, but gains by dealing with a hand that has no obvious answer. In addition, if a double is negative then other bids can be put to work. For instance, if 1♥—2♣— Dble is for take-out, responder can give extra definition to the meaning of the bids 2♦ and 2♠. In a sequence starting 1♦—1♥ a double could show four spades and a bid of 1♠ promise five or more. Without intervention, i.e. 1♦—Pass—1♠, we don't know if responder has four or more spades, but it doesn't seem to create any real difficulty.

If you open the bidding, your left hand opponent intervenes and the bidding is passed back to you, you would pass contentedly with a minimum. Should you re-open, partner can be sure of plus values of some kind. Playing negative doubles, you have to re-open on many minimum hands, in case partner was fixed by the intervention. Many take this to the ridiculous extreme of stating that after an opening, an intervention and two passes, opener is COMPELLED to bid again. This is no better than trying to see through fog. I strongly recommend that when opponents are playing negative doubles, you enquire as to just what extent passes are forcing. If they are completely forcing and you are sitting in the fourth seat (1♥—2♣—Pass—?), just pass, wait for them to arrive in the swamp, and then bury them.

Even I admit that there are some hands when a negative double is of advantage. For example, after an opening of a minor suit and an intervention of 1♠, a take-out double will be of far greater use than a business double. The pre-emptive effect of the spade overcall can best be dealt with by this conventional aid. Most players would also agree with using double for take-out of jump overcalls up to a certain level.

(d) Responsive and Competitive Doubles

These can be lumped together for practical purposes. Tremendous strides have been made in developing competitive accuracy by using the double as a positive aid to bidding. To have to forego the pleasure of doubling the enemy for business in situations where they have announced their readiness to be doubled, is a small price to pay for greater definition. A perfect example is the simple sequence 1♥—Dble—2♥—Dble.

You can see where the expression Responsive double comes from. Who wants to use the second double for cash when there are multitudes of hands that would like to bid something, but know not what? Of course if you can make a sensible bid then you should always do so, because one inference of a responsive double is that you had no other convenient bid available.

The immense increase in the subtlety of meanings arising from the use of competitive doubles recommends it to all aspiring partnerships. One is tempted to say perspiring partnerships, because work on the meaning of various sequences is vital. There are so many grey areas that could become black and white without too much strain on the understanding of even moderate but keen pairs.

How would you interpret the double in the sequence 1♥—1♠—2♥—Dble? If you assume it to be punitive, you are arguing that you can get a reasonable profit in the long term by doubling the enemy in a low level contract of their own choice. If you adopt it as a 'keep the conversation going partner' device you will have no trouble with a hand such as:

♠ J 4   ♥ 8 3   ♦ K Q 9 3   ♣ K Q 9 4 2

So doubles of opponents who have VOLUNTARILY raised a suit are for take out, but we must fix a level. Up to 3♥ is efficient, but it would be better to say that up to 3♥ the double is for take-out, and that doubles of voluntary raises at a higher level offer more option but with the same over-riding attitude — I would like to bid, but I do not know what. Here are a few examples from real life, and decide how you would understand the final bid in the following auctions.

(1)	South	West	North	East	(2)	South	West	North	East
	1♥	1♠	2♥	Dble		1♥	1♠	2♥	Dble
	Pass	3♣	Pass	3♦		Pass	2♠	Pass	3♣

(3)	South	West	North	East	(4)	South	West	North	East
	1♥	1♠	2♥	Dble		1♥	1♠	2♥	3♣/3♦
	Pass	3♦	Pass	3♠					

(5)	South	West	North	East
	1♥	Pass	2♥	Pass
	Pass	2♠	3♥	Dble

(1) East asked you to bid. You were able to show a second suit and yet you hear of another. East preferred spades to clubs, but wished to show diamonds en route. Something like:

$$♠ Q 9 \quad ♥ J 4 2 \quad ♦ A Q J 10 4 2 \quad ♣ 6 4.$$

(2) East heard you say that you were only interested in spades but still removed, so he must have something like:

$$♠ J \quad ♥ 5 3 \quad ♦ K Q 10 8 6 \quad ♣ K Q J 3 2.$$

(3) East preferred spades to diamonds yet did not give you an immediate raise, so he must have clubs

$$♠ J 4 2 \quad ♥ 5 3 \quad ♦ J 3 2 \quad ♣ A K J 10 8.$$

(4) The absence of the competitive double clearly states that (a) East does not have both minors, (b) does not have a good minor with spade tolerance; thus he must have a one-suited hand.

(5) Common sense suggests that the bid of 2♠ denies support for the minors. Still and all, the double is for take-out. So partner must be prepared to battle on, probably with reasonable spade support and good high card content. Perhaps:

$$♠ A J 4 \quad ♥ K 6 3 \quad ♦ A 9 8 6 \quad ♣ J 10 7.$$

When this actual hand occurred, West could 'see' what East held and passed to collect a 500 penalty. You see, sometimes you can pick up the penalties which the business doublers miss, and your opponents are bewildered by how you came to double them in the other room.

Another use of the competitive double comes after three suits have been bid, such as 1♥–1♠–2♣–Dble. We gave up this particular double for business at the time bridge became a game of intelligence. It should show the unbid suit and tolerance for partner's suit. Some pairs vary the treatment depending on whether or not the opposing 2♣ was forcing; but this will only tax your brain for no reason. Have a bash at some more interpretations.

(1)	South	West	North	East
	1♥	1♠	2♣	Dble
	Pass	2♠	Pass	3♦

(2)	South	West	North	East
	1♥	1♠	2♣	Dble
	3♣	Pass	Pass	Dble

(3)	South	West	North	East
	1♥	1♠	2♣	Dble
	2♥	3♦	Pass	3♠

(4)	South	West	North	East
	1♥	1♠	2♣	2♦

(1) Having already shown diamonds and spade tolerance, East must be making a forward move with good diamonds, something akin to:

    ♠ A 2   ♥ 4 2   ♦ A K J 6 5 3 2   ♣ J 4.

(2) As the double is systematically for take out and the first double specified diamonds with spade tolerance, East is clearly refusing to sell out, but with no clear cut bid available. It could be another 'take the money' opportunity,

    ♠ K 4 . ♥ J 10 6 3   ♦ A K J 4   ♣ J 10 5

(3) You chose East's announced suit but still he prefers spades. So he must have a genuine spade raise — with good diamonds:

    ♠ K 10 8   ♥ 9 8   ♦ A K J 10   ♣ 10 8 7 3.

You can see that it makes for an easy life and a simple road to gathering cash or match points.

(4) Obvious. East has diamonds — and is not interested in your flaming spades.

To introduce competitive doubles to your style will give a whole new dimension to bidding in competition. As Norman Squire the great theorist would say, we have fished a little but it's certain that there are many depths unplumbed, and rich hauls available for the assiduous fishermen.

(e) Alder Three Bids

Pre-emptive bidding has perhaps changed a little in style over the years. I once went on record as saying that the best defence to opening pre-empts was a take-out double. It is certainly the best in terms of economy, but my reasons were because the pendulum had swung away from the infamous Meredith pre-empts (J—x—x—x—x and a sprig of four leaf clover) to a more secure type. When fashions change, so must we, to keep up with the field. The following scheme licensed by Philip Alder (pinching some of the ideas from myself and Terence Reese) incorporates obstructive machinery with some technical advance.

3♣.   Natural. Can be used as a standard pre-empt; or semi-constructive, promising two of the top three honours or — more of use to the strong club merchants — to show a minimum opening bid with seven clubs. You pays your money . . . .

3♦.   An opening pre-empt in either major suit. It makes the opponents' problems more acute when they are not sure which suit they are bidding against.
Responder bids 3♥ if he would have passed an opening 3♥, or bids 3♠ if he would have passed an opening 3♠ but would have raised an opening 3♥ to four.
All game bids are to play. (3NT/4♥/4♠/5♣/5♦)
A 4♣ response is a slam try. Opener can then bid 4♦ to show interest, or signs off in his major if he is without ambition.
A 4♦ response simply asks opener to bid game in whichever major suit he holds.

3♥.   This is a pre-empt in either minor. Responses are in line with those to 3♦. As many players nowadays use an opening four of a minor to show a good major pre-empt, one can regain the use of a minor suit pre-empt.

3♠.   This replaces the standard gambling 3NT, which should show a solid minor suit with no high card outside except for the odd queen. The immediate advantage is that when 3NT is the right contract, it is played from the right side. Responses are the same as to an opening 3NT. i.e. All game bids are to play, except that a bid of 5♦ asks opener to pass or bid 6♣ if that is his suit. e.g.:

♠ A K x x   ♥ A K Q x x   ♦ x   ♣ x x x

4♣ is a bail out, and opener should pass or correct to 4♦. 4♦ requests information about singletons. Opener bids 4♥/4♠ with the specified singleton, 4NT with none, and five of his suit with a singleton in the other minor.

3NT.   Unless used as natural, this needs to be licensed. Useful to the artificial boys who can, for instance, use it to show 25—27 points in a 4—3—3—3 hand. Though rare, it at least means that all other sequences deny 4—3—3—3.

(f) Responses to Standard Pre-empts

Years ago, one of the Sharples sadists asked me what I would bid after an opening 3♠ by partner with:

♠ A 7   ♥ K 6   ♦ A K Q J 10 4   ♣ A 6 2

Before I had time to toss a mental coin he added, 'what would you do if you held:

♠ A 7 2   ♥ K 6   ♦ A K Q J 10 4   ♣ A 6'.

The difference, of course, is the extra trump. Anyway, the answer was easy.

After three of a major, 4♣ by responder is conventional, and asks opener to value his trump suit facing A–x or K–x, and bid six if it is completely solid. Should responder instead bid five of the major it would ask opener to value his trumps facing A–x–x or K–x–x. All other bids are normal slam tries, except that we know that responder did not choose the conventional path. The first had cropped up in an International match. 3♠–4♣–6♠–6NT. Duck soup.

One can arrange many things around the theme. 3♠–4♣/–4♦/ 5♦, could show a one loser trump suit with second round diamond control/first round diamond control. You paid for the book, but the aim is to make you do, and enjoy doing, some work, so here is a nice uncomplicated area in which you can demonstrate your ingenuity.

(g) After an Opening Four of a Major

It has become normal for players to use opening bids of 4♣/4♦ to show pretty solid openings in the majors. It is also normal for an opening pre-empt to deny two aces, or rather two first round controls. We all bend the rules from time to time, but we do it bearing in mind the risk. Assuming that the opening 4♥/4♠ is sensible, responder should not embark on a slam hunt with less than two outside suits controlled.

Space is limited, so we must use it to full advantage. The best approach therefore is to bid the suit below the one that is uncontrolled. Thus 4♥–Pass–4♠ would deny club control. 4♥–Pass–5♣ would deny diamond control, etc.

Opener should not accept the try without the requisite control. Should he be fortunate to have it, there is still more than one way it could be shown. So it could go:

4♥–4♠–5♣,	I have a singleton club (or king)
4♥–4♠–6♣,	I have a void club (or ace – once in a decade)
4♥–4♠–5♦/5♠.	I have a second round club control, but bad trumps
4♥–4♠–6♥	I have second round club control, with good trumps.

A raise of opener's major to the five level must have an explicit meaning. Time has not suggested any improvement on the old meaning that there are no losers outside the trump suit. Over an opening 4♠, a typical hand for 5♠ would be:

♠ 9   ♥ A K 7   ♦ A K 10 9 6   ♣ A K 6 4

(h) After 2♣ −2♦−3♥/3♠

After an opening bid of 2♣ and a negative response of 2♦, a jump to 3♥ or 3♠ shows a solid suit. Once in a while responder will have an ace which he must cue bid, but assuming no ace opposite the opening, the following treatment is then recommended. A raise to four of the major will show no values, while 3NT will show some working values. Now opener can use a conventional bid of 4♣ to ask for kings. If you hold any particular king then this will be cue bid, if you hold any two kings then you jump in the higher ranking, and if you have none, you return to partner's suit. Opener can now bid 4NT asking for queens. Again you would cue bid one specific queen, jump in the higher ranking of two, and bid six of partner's suit with three.

This is a very simple piece of machinery which leads to tremendous accuracy on the rare occasions when these hands crop up. There is an automatic corollary advantage that if the bidding should take a different course then responder can get a very clear idea of what opener wants. Suppose that the bidding were to proceed:

$$2♣ −2♦/3♠−3NT/4♥$$

What can 4♥ mean? Opener could have asked about kings and subsequently about queens; so he must be directing your attention specifically to the heart suit. Over 4♥, with Q−x−x you would jump to five of opener's suit. If not you sign off in 4♠, and if opener then bids 5♥ it is almost as clear as if he were holding his hand facing you. Opener is asking if you have a doubleton heart, providing of course that you have enough spades to ruff the heart losers. The following hand, which cropped up in a national team tournament not so long ago, illustrates the scheme in action:

♠ A K Q J 10 x x x   ♥ A K x   ♦ A x   ♣ −

The bidding proceeded:

$$2♣−2♦/3♠−3NT/4♣−4♦/4NT−5♥/7♠$$

(i) Three Way (Fruit Machine) Swiss

After an opening bid of one of a major, a bid of 4♣ shows a good raise to four, including one of the following:

(1) Two aces and a singleton,

or (2) Two aces and the king of trumps,

or (3) Three aces.

If opener is interested to find out which is responder's holding he can inquire by bidding 4♦. With two aces and a singleton responder would then sue bid the singleton, with two aces and the king of trumps. he returns to the trump suit, and with three aces he bids 4NT.

If after the opening bid of one of a major responder bids 4♦, he shows a high card raise to four which does not include any of the above hands, a bid we call a 'pudding' raise.

In both these cases responder will have general rather than specific values, which would be more efficiently shown by a delayed game raise. It is important to bear in mind that all these bids show a hand not strong enough to make an immediate force on the first round.

After an opening one of a major, 4♦ would show a good (high card) raise to four of the major — without any of the pre-requisites of the 4♣ response.

(j) Crowhurst

A sequence such as 1♥—1♠—1NT would appear to be fairly closely defined, however, the kind of hand that rebids 1NT can vary considerably both in what I would call working strength and in suitability for various strains. Thus the Crowhurst convention is a way of gaining the information required in deciding the right level and the right strain. The convention arises after a sequence of one of a suit, a response of one of a suit, a rebid of one no-trump and then 2♣ by responder. This is the conventional bid. Most partnerships would insist that the 1NT rebid should carry a fairly narrow range, but nonetheless you will find this addition to your bidding armoury very useful. For the increasing number of players who like to play a wider range of no-trump rebid, then to have a way of more narrowly defining the opener's shape and strength is vital. In fact it is fairly common for a sequence like 1♥—1♠—1NT to carry a range of between 12 and 16 points. There are several ideas as to how best use the convention, but the way that I play it has proved to be very efficient and is as follows.

2♣ — simply asks the question. Let's assume that the bidding has started 1♥—1♠/1NT—2♣. Opener now has the duty to give responder more information about the hand type. All suit bids at the two level i.e. 2♦/♥/♠ will be regarded as showing a hand type in the minimum range. In our case we play the range as between 15 and 17 and 2♦ would show a minimum type hand without five hearts or three spades, 2♥ to show a hand in minimum range with five hearts, 2♠ to show a hand in minimum range with three card spade support. 2NT would show a hand that was maximum and would suggest that the partnership proceed to game.

Thereafter responder can still probe, should he desire, for the best possible game. A sequence such as 1♥—1♠/1NT—2♣/2NT—3♣ /♦ would now be regarded as a natural bid (presumably responder would have five spades and four of the minor) and still be unsure of the right final destination. If responder bid 3♥ it would show three card heart support and would suggest an alternative contract to opener. A rebid of 3♠ would show that the spades were at least five and again give the opener options. One can also add to the vocabulary by allowing the opener to jump with maximum hands as for instance 1♥—1♠/1NT—2♣/3♠. This would show a hand in the maximum range with a particularly high degree of suitability for suit play, thus a hand such as the following:

♠ A 7 2   ♥ A J 6 3   ♦ A 8 6 4   ♣ K 2

With so little in the way of tenaces, the high card content, and the doubleton it is very useful to be able to stress to responder that it is a maximum hand of this type. Make the hand into the following:

♠ 7 3 2   ♥ K Q 10 6   ♦ A Q 10   ♣ A J 2

and then it would be better to bid 2NT after 2♣, to show a maximum hand. Should responder, as mentioned earlier, feel that there is some doubt about no-trumps being the right denomination he can still probe and then you can show the three card spade support. We have added a gimmick in that with a hand such as:

♠ A 6 4 2   ♥ K 10 3   ♦ A K 4   ♣ K 7 2

not being allowed to open 1♣ for systemic reasons, we would open 1♦. The reasoning is fairly straightforward. If one opens 1♠ one finds that all too frequently the suit is raised with inadequate support and the suit quality is so bad that one only finds out in the post-mortem that no-trumps was the best spot. To get back to the point, we open the hand 1♦ and should partner respond 1♠ we would still rebid 1NT, feeling that it is less likely to lead to confusion in describing the hand type and strength accurately than to support spades. It is a matter of conjecture as to how many spades one should bid, but however many you decide to bid there is no doubt that the responder will get an impression that you had a shapely rather than a balanced hand. Should responder now bid 2♣, Crowhurst, we would jump to 3NT to show precisely this 4—3—3—3 hand with four card support for partner and a maximum point count. Others could adapt the same machinery to show a complete maximum 4—3—3—3 hand with three card support for partner. For consistency it is a good idea to agree that all bids at the two level are non-forcing even after Crowhurst. For example a sequence such as 1♥—1♠/1NT—2♣/2♦ — 2♠, while obviously encouraging, opener can pass; as he would also be able to pass a bid of 2♥. All bids at the three level, however, would be forcing, thus 1♥—1♠/1NT—2♣/2♦—3♣ would be natural, showing spades and clubs and a hand that still insisted on being in game despite opener's minimum values. It is essential that one then adopts a general policy of bidding a hand such as:

♠ K 10 7 2   ♥ 6 2   ♦ 7   ♣ K 10 8 5 4 2

After a 1♥ opening bid I think that we would all agree that one must bid 1♠ should opener now bid 1NT, in my style 15—17, showing a balanced hand in any style, a jump to 3♣ now would show precisely this hand type, a four card spade suit and a longer club suit and it would be a complete sign off.

Another type of situation where a Crowhurst-type of machinery is of use is after a protective 1NT, for instance the bidding is opened on your right with 1♠ and is passed round to your partner who protects with a bid of 1NT. As you have read, it is my suggestion that this bid should carry a fairly wide range, thus it becomes very important that a 2♣-type machinery to enquire about the range is a vital part of accurate bidding. We follow the same basic principles as mentioned earlier; 2♦, would just show a minimum hand with no major suit, 2♥/♠ would show a minimum hand with a four card major, 2NT would show a hand that was in the middle of the range and thus encouraging but not completely game forcing, and the 2♣ enquirer could then, if he so wished, proceed with the investigation; all bids at the three level would be forcing to game and natural. Thus 1♠—Pass—Pass—1NT/Pass—2♣—Pass—3♦ would show that the no-trump bidder was in the top range, had a diamond suit and insisted on being in game. This would still leave the partnership the opportunity of investigating a possible 4—4 heart fit.

(k) Coping with Strong Club Openings

In this day and age with an ever increasing number of artificial methods being used largely based on a strong club opening bid, it is becoming of ever increasing necessity to disrupt the free flow of information between the opponents. Some systems are so sophisticated with multitudinous asking bids that given a free run they can almost certainly get to the right contract. Thus it is very important to somehow break up this free flowing conversation. My own invented, disruptive convention against strong club systems came about when I watched the last world championships that the Italians won. Up until that time we had always adopted, as most people do, a system of two suited overcalls to try to pre-empt the opponents out of their rightful contract, or at least make it difficult for them to discover it. It soon became apparent that after a Precision Club opening bid it was vital to be able to bid at the one level in the natural sense, because already the opponents are deprived of some of their conventional aids and on the many occasions when partner was able to put a further spoke into the wheel by raising the suit, they lost all their ability to make asking bids. So I came back to England to tell the team that we had to abandon our two-suited style of bidding because it was so vital to get into the bidding at the one level.

I think again that it is an important issue to have complete partnership agreement that the object of the exercise is to disrupt. There is no premium on gearing your bidding to getting to contracts that you can bid and make after an opening strong club. Thus our tendency and our recommendation is to assume that partner is bidding on a load of seaweed, because it is relatively safe to bid at a low level on seaweed. From this base of disruption the following method was concocted.

Amsbury vs Strong Club

After an opening bid of 1♣ : Dble shows both major suits.

1♦/♥/♠ are all natural showing the suit.

1NT shows a non-touching two-
suiter, i.e. hearts and clubs or
diamonds and spades.
2NT shows both the minor suits.

The interesting and quite fun-making part of the method comes
with 2—level bids. After an opening bid of 1♣, suit bids at the two
level have three possible meanings, as follows.

(1) They are natural and equivalent to a weak jump overcall
     in the suit just bid.
(2) You are bidding the singleton, having the other three suits;
     there is a very high degree of safety in having three suits.
(3) You are bidding a non-existent suit but have two touching
     suits in your hand excluding the suit you have just bid and
     the suit above it. The reason for this will be explained.

You will have noticed that one can show majors and minors in
two different ways, for instance after 1♣ I could overcall 2♦, with
hearts and spades, or I could overcall 2♥ with clubs and diamonds.
The reason for having this dual way of showing the suits is that
one can double 1♣ with as little as two four-card major suits, as it
is highly unlikely that you will come to any great harm at the one
level in a major. Also it is very useful on the occasion that partner
has a major suit fit, that he can raise the level high very quickly.
The same applies to the minor suits. If I can bid 2NT to show both
minors with some reasonable length partner again can raise the
ante very quickly. The bidding thereafter can get a little confusing
for both sides, but bearing in mind the opponents known strength
they are much more likely to be on the wrong end of the bad
result. Should left-hand opponent double your two level overcall
and it is passed back to you, you would pass if it happened to be
your suit and feel grateful that you had been able to sacrifice at
such a low level, redouble to show that you had bid your singleton and let partner bail out (sometimes with a jump into one of
your known suits), or bid the lower of the two touching suits and
leave partner to judge which of the two suits to play in. It is for
this reason that one cannot bid, at the two level, the lower of the

two suits because there is no way that you can subsequently show the other suit.

Sometimes partner will want to know which of the hand types you are holding for reasons of pre-emption. In general he will assume the suit to be natural and will pass on the assumption that you will not be too distressed at going off a few undoubled, but there are hands when partner will know that some fit must exist and he can then enquire about your hand-type by bidding 2NT. The original renegade would then, in simple enough style, rebid the suit bid to show that it was a natural overcall, bid any other suit to show that suit and the next suit up, and bid 3NT to state that he had bid his singleton.

Apart from the odd occasion when your partner is strong enough to envisage game despite the opening strong club bid, you will notice that no-trumps is being played from the right side and in any case he is well able to judge the best possible strain. You can see that it is important that an assumption is made that the bid is weak and disruptive; it means that one can enter the fray with much greater frequency. One trap to look out for is when the bidding starts 1♣ on your left, pass from partner, 1♦ on your right and you feel inclined to adopt this machinery. One must bear in mind that in keeping with all good style, one always passes after a strong 1♣ with a strong hand so before you leap into action, bear in mind that your partner may have passed 1♣ with a very strong hand and he is not going to be too pleased to try and unscramble the ensuing auction when you can have any one of three possible hand types. When I first put the idea to my partner, Tony Sowter, having played it a fair amount myself, his comment was that it was a system that would work very well against children. This may strike you the same way. Just a couple of days later I happened to be playing against him playing a strong club system. I was partnering his wife playing our strong club system with this particular defence in operation and Tony opened the bidding with 1♣, I overcalled with 2♦, (one of the many varieties), his partner doubled, as is usual in negative style to show values, my partner raised to 4♦ and now Tony had the dilemma of sorting out the problem of dealing with a strong hand that was largely composed of A–K–

Q—x—x—x in diamonds. My partner was able to jump to 4♦ with some comfort, especially non-vulnerable against vulnerable, having a 5—4—3—1 distribution. To their credit, Tony and partner did manage to find their spade fit and played in 5♠ and when we found that, on opening the travelling score sheet the whole room had scored 620 and they were minus 100, I could not resist commenting to Tony: 'Perhaps you're right, I ought to give this system up, it does only work against children.' Joking apart, we have found that, after five years, this method does create almost insoluble problems for players of the highest rank.

Chapter 15.

What Would You Bid Now?

The object of this chapter is to find out how closely you have read the book. The hands that are shown all occured in real life and while it could be argued that they could have been bid accurately to the best final contract by other methods, you will see in part two of the chapter that the best contract can be reached with the maximum of fluency. Again one must give praise to the amount of hard work put into the natural bidding vocabulary by Bob and Jim Sharples and Jack Marx over the years. I would reiterate that on big hand bidding, and most of these hands are on the large side, it is vital to look ahead, it is also vital to think back to the bid that your partner made on the previous round and the bid that he made on the round before. Another tip that was passed on to me years ago was that when you find yourself about to bid a slam, it is sometimes a good idea to reconstruct the hand that you believe your partner to hold and then bid it as if you really could see it. Very often just this simple exercise will show beyond all doubt that your partner cannot hold the hand that you want him to hold.

	Partner	You
Hand 1		
♠ K 6		
♥ Q J 8 7 3	1♦	1♥
♦ Q 9 6 4	1♠	?
♣ Q 8		
Hand 2		
♠ —		
♥ A J 7 3		
♦ 6 4	1♦	2♣
♣ Q J 10 9 8 6 3	2♠	?

		Partner	You
Hand 3			
♠	—		1♦
♥	Q 7 5		
♦	A K 9 6 5	1♥	2♣
♣	K Q J 8 6	2♠	?

		Partner	You
Hand 4			
♠	A 8 7 4		
♥	K Q 8 6	1♦	1♥
♦	A	2♥	?
♣	K Q J 6		

		Partner	You
Hand 5			
♠	Q J 7		
♥	K 10 6	1♦	?
♦	J 10 6		
♣	A K 8 3		

		Partner	You
Hand 6			
♠	A Q 8 3		
♥	Q J 10 9 8 6 4		1♥
♦	—	2♦	?
♣	Q 2		

		Partner	You
Hand 7			
♠	A 6 2		
♥	J 10 8 7 4	1♦	1♥
♦	A K 8 2	1♠	2♣
♣	6	2♦	?

		Partner	You
Hand 8			
♠	A 7		
♥	J 4	Pass	1♦
♦	K J 9 6 5	3♣	?
♣	A Q 8 6		

3♣ shows a good raise to 3♦ and a club suit

	Partner	You
Hand 9		
♠ 6	1♣	1♦
♥ 9 6 4	1♠	3♣
♦ A K Q 10	3♥	4♣
♣ Q 8 7 4 2	4♠	?

	Partner	You
Hand 10		
♠ A		
♥ A K J 8 7 4		2♥
♦ 8 4	3♥	?
♣ A K 9 5		

2♥ is forcing, promising eight or more tricks
3♥ shows the values for game and is unlimited.

In answering the questions it would be a good idea to analyse your thinking processes to see how closely they tie up with mine.

PART TWO

			The bidding	
			Partner	You
Hand 1				
♠ K 6	♠ A 10 7 3		1♦	1♥
♥ Q J 8 7 3	♥ —		1♠	3♦
♦ Q 9 6 4	♦ K J 10 5 2		4♣	4♦
♣ Q 8	♣ A K 3 2		4♠	6♦

It would seem that in Britain we are the last bastion of natural bidders that regard jump preference as non-forcing. It has been clearly established that there are many ways of bidding and also you must all have experienced the frequency of tangles that occur at the table when a hand is not clearly defined, especially at the point of the responder's second bid. The jump preference to 3♦ describes the hand admirably in saying that you have a raise of 1♦ to 3♦ and you have shown your heart suit. 4♣ can only be interpreted at this time as a try for game. Your hand does not look to be particularly good so it makes sense to sign off in 4♦. However the 4♠ bid by partner makes it clear that he was always interested in a slam on your bidding and so now one can look more lovingly at the king doubleton in spades and the reasonable quality of the trumps and can look back at the fact that only the round before we expressed the disinclination even to go to game, thus we must now trust partner and bid the slam.

			The bidding	
			Partner	You
Hand 2				
♠ A J 7 6	♠ —		1♦	2♣
♥ K 8 4	♥ A J 7 3		2♠	3♣
♦ A K 10 9 3	♦ 6 4		3♥	5♣
♣ K	♣ Q J 10 9 8 6 3		6♣	

After a reverse bid, in old fashioned method, a simple rebid of a suit, as here a rebid of 3♣, would be regarded as non-forcing. However, time has led most players to believe that after a two-level response a reverse bid should be forcing to the four level and if you have been compelled to bid at the two level on some load of garbage, but made safe by some great length in your suit, then you have to struggle on to the four level in your suit at which stage partner can pass. Many hands occur, nonetheless, where after a reverse you would like to show your partner that you have a very good suit and it becomes very contorted and tangled if you start waffling through a fourth suit sequence. Even if the bid is played as non-forcing I still think it is right. The hand is not likely to make 3NT unless partner makes some further move over 3♣. When he makes this further move of 3♥ I think it would be very unwise to bid no-trumps. We do have a considerable amount of value to spare and one may consider raising 3♥ to 4♥ hopefully to show some length and also hoping that partner will assume that you have the ace, however the jump to 5♣ says all this and is almost certainly going to be a safe contract. I think that you would all agree that the raise to 6♣ with the singleton king now becomes completely automatic despite the fact that in a very strong field, not one pair out of forty managed to bid this slam. When the hand was given to a top class natural pair to bid they produced the bidding sequence shown and sailed into the lay-down slam.

The bidding

		You	Partner
Hand 3			
♠ 10 9 6	♠ —	1♦	1♥
♥ A K J 6	♥ Q 7 5	2♣	2♠
♦ Q 10 8	♦ A K 9 6 5	4♣	4♦
♣ A 7 4	♣ K Q J 8 6	4♥	5♣
		5♠	7♣

At the point when partner bid 2♠, the fourth suit, he had at least the values to play in 2NT and thus it is incumbent upon us to make some strong bid. We would all agree that the hand looks highly unsuitable for playing in no-trumps so we are left with the choice of jumping in either clubs or hearts. There is something to be said for jumping to 4♥ but it in no way stresses the quality of the minor suits and who knows, as happened here, you may get the chance to show that heart support. When partner bids 5♣ he is obviously agreeing, having previously supported diamonds, that he is prepared to play in game at the five level and perhaps more, and thus you as West should see the enormous potential of the hand and realise that the slam is on. It is a good general principle that one should never just bid a slam if it costs nothing to make a grand slam try. I am constantly telling young players to stop looking for the pot of gold at the end of the rainbow, and it is worth reminding you again of the words of the great American player Barry Crane, never play the 'if' game, i.e. 'if partner has this' and 'if partner has that'. But if it costs nothing to find out whether or not partner holds just the right cards, then it must be the right thing to do. Thus 5♠ clearly states the hand — spade control, heart fit and two good minor suits, all this bearing in mind that the bidding started 1♦—1♥ and then only 2♣, so the opening bidder was limited both by the failure to jump on the second round and by the failure to open with a two bid. The whole hand should be an open book now and the jump to 7♣ becomes quite clear and also suggests that clubs may be a sounder contract than diamonds.

be a sounder alternative contract than diamonds.

Hand 4

		The bidding	
		You	Partner
♠ K 6	♠ A 8 7 4	1♥	1♦
♥ A J 9	♥ K Q 8 6	2♠	2♥
♦ J 10 9 8 6 5	♦ A	4♣	3♣
♣ A 7	♣ K Q J 6	4NT	4♥
		6♥	5♥

At the point when you bid 2♠ partner can only assume that you were making a try for game, 3♣ now shows values in clubs and is encouraging. You now bid 4♣ with both possibilities of agreeing a suit that partner may hold and suggesting a slam, and partner back-pedals by signing off in 4♥. With the inference that partner has a long, not very good diamond suit, because he did not open 1NT, which we agree as standard should show 12—14 balanced points, we can just about see that he must have exactly the right cards to make the slam in hearts a good proposition.

		The bidding	
		Partner	You
Hand 5			
♠ A 6	♠ Q J 7		1♦
♥ Q J 7 4	♥ K 10 6	3NT	
♦ A K Q 6 5 3	♦ J 10 6	5♣	4♥
♣ 6	♣ A K 8 3		6♦

The auction really is a model of economy; the important point is that the leap to 3NT by responder is frowned upon by openers. The reason for this is that they always feel that they are left in the air. However there is no need ever to get this feeling if the partnership agrees that the bid should have a specific meaning. In other words it should be a hand of almost identifiable strength and shape, thus after a bid of one of a minor, a jump to 3NT would say, 'I have 13—15 high card points, a fair collection of aces and kings, I do not have a four card major but I do have a guard in all unbid suits'. The 4♥ bid was not an attempt to play in 4♥ but the clearest slam try that he could make; it showed his probable shape and announced at least the values to play in 4NT or 5♦. From our point of view the slam now becomes a very good proposition provided that there are not two spade losers or two aces missing; to ask for aces would not be regarded as Blackwood but as a sign-off, thus we are left with the try of 5♣, a cue bid. I think that again we can all agree that partner has a very easy problem in deciding whether or not to bid the slam, especially when we bear in mind that partner knows we have top cards in the majors and a balanced hand.

Hand 6

			The bidding	
			Partner	You
♠ —	♠ A Q 8 3		2♦	1♥
♥ A K 5 3	♥ Q J 10 9 8 6 4		4♣	3♥
♦ Q J 10 9 8 5	♦ —		5♠	4♥
♣ A K 9	♣ Q 2		7♥	5NT

The first problem with the rebid is in wondering whether or not to introduce the spade suit. Of course, in principle a reverse only announces the values to play in your first suit at the next high level if partner should prefer it, however, as we have previously examined, after a two level response a reverse is normally game forcing, thus you abandon the idea and make a bid he can pass, whilst showing him your great playing strength. The 4♣ bid in all good modern style is not logical, in the natural sense, thus it is a cue bid agreeing hearts. With a void diamond and a fairly minimum hand without top trumps East rightly signs off. West of course was always intending to play in 6♥; as mentioned before, he can settle the whole matter quite easily by jumping to 5♠ passing many messages: (1) He has a void spade; (2) He has a very powerful hand and thus his values must be in the outher suits. From East's point of view, as long as West holds the ace and king of hearts, it is certain that there will be a way of disposing of any second club loser, thus he has only to ask whether his partner has two of the top three honours in hearts. Many may ask why West did not force over 1♥? Again, I can only quote from my own experience that it is very unwise to force in a suit that does not include the ace or king. Partners always assume, and there is a certain amount of validity in their thinking, that when you force in a suit it contains a top card. As we can see, it is very easy subsequently to tell partner that you were always on a slam hunt and it is then very often that partner can work out why you did not force in the first place if this is the case.

		The bidding	
		Partner	You
Hand 7			
♠ Q J 7 5	♠ A 6 2	1♦	1♥
♥ —	♥ J 10 8 7 4	1♠	2♣
♦ Q J 9 7 6 5	♦ A K 8 2	2♦	4♦
♣ A K 4	♣ 6	4♥	4♠
		6♦	

In the examination of fourth suit bidding it was recommended, and hopefully you were convinced, that responder, after bidding the fourth suit, subsequently supports the opener, then this bid should be forcing for one round. Thus it would appear that the jump to 4♦ was unnecessary and space consuming. One of the themes that crops up over and over again is that the consumption of space is in itself not a fault in bidding provided that the message sent is explicit. It was recommended that if after bidding the fourth suit you then make an unnecessary jump in one of opener's suits it would state that your values, as here, are about game values and that all your cards are known to be working, not the odd queens in suits that could be useless. West had to find out that you had some spade control, thus the cue bid of 4♥, but as soon as he found this out from your cue bid of 4♠ it was obvious that your values were top diamond, top spade and nothing in hearts that was wasted. If you had a little more strength in hearts you would, you remember, have forced over 1♦ immediately. You could not regard K J 10 x x as values that were definitely working so partner can almost see your hand.

			The bidding	
			You	Partner
Hand 8				
♠ A 7	♠ 10 4 3 2			Pass
♥ J 4	♥ —		1♦	3♣
♦ K J 9 6 5	♦ A Q 8 7		4♠	5NT
♣ A Q 8 6	♣ K J 9 7 3		7♣	7♦

I would not blame you if you felt that the bidding sequence proceeded in leaps and bounds as though you were a pair of demented water buffaloes. Every bid is, however, exactly right in the context of our earlier thinking. Having passed, it is such a vital use of an otherwise wasted bid to show that you have not just a raise of partner's suit to a specific level, but a raise of a specific type with values in a specific place. Thus 3♣ tells not just that you have a 1♦–3♦ bid but that this bid includes a club suit. As soon as West gets this information it is obvious that he is going to proceed to game. If he is going on to game he can also investigate the possibility of you holding just the right cards to make a slam, thus the jump to 4♠ again, as in previous examples, passes more than one message: (1) I have first round spade control. (2) I am implying very strongly that I have two losing hearts. (3) I have a big club fit with you. Looking at it from East's point of view, if partner has the ace of spades, two losing hearts, obviously a reasonable diamond suit and a good club fit, all he needs to know is the quality of the club support; does he have the ace and the queen? So he employs the 5NT grand slam force to ascertain the location of the two top honours. Having got the right information he then transfers to the logical grand slam — the obvious reason being that heart ruffs can be taken by the hand with the shorter trumps and hopefully there will be a discard available as well on the fifth club. When this hand occurred with two world class pairs in opposition, one pair did arrive in a minor suit slam but the other pair could not get past game.

The bidding

	Partner	You
	1♣	1♦
Hand 9	1♠	1♠
♠ A K 10 5 ♠ 6	3♥	4♣
♥ A 10 2 ♥ 9 6 4	4♠	5♦
♦ 6 ♦ A K Q 10	7♣	
♣ A K 10 9 6 ♣ Q 8 7 4 2		

It would do no harm to repeat that we must always put the horse before the cart and assume that bids made below game are in an effort to find out whether a game is on or, alternatively, if partner knows that there is some game on, what the right game should be. After 3♥, East could logically feel that he had no more to say other than to bid 4♣, though some more optimistic characters may even cue bid 4♠ before returning to clubs. When West makes a clear cut slam try of 4♠, bearing in mind our adopted style that we tend to show our hand pattern, he is making the slam try with a known shortage in diamonds and so he must have a quite gigantic hand. Certainly we are going to accept a slam try with a singleton spade and the extra trump and in this case does it cost anything to bid 5♦. He also knows that we know of his shortage of diamonds and thus we must be telling him about the quality of the suit. From his point of view now, with nine cards at least in the minor suits he can see that losing hearts in his hand can be disposed of on our diamonds and losing spades can be ruffed in our hand. The solution is ridiculously simple if you think about it. To finish off, one last hand:

		The bidding	
		Partner	You
Hand 10			2♥
♠ J 8 4	♠ A	3♥	5♣
♥ Q 10 6	♥ A K J 8 7 4	5♦	5♠
♦ A 9 3	♦ 8 4	7♣	
♣ Q J 8 4	♣ A K 9 5		

I introduce this hand as yet another application of a jump bid that can be used by any pair, even those playing artificial methods. The hand was bid in the manner shown by Bob and Jim Sharples in the final of one of the many tournaments that they have won over the years and 2♥–3♥, in keeping with our discussion, did not promise an ace, it promised just good heart support and the values to raise at least to game. With the suit bid and agreed, a jump in a new suit, as here 5♣, guarantees a four card suit headed by the ace and king at least. The 5♦ cue bid was what East wanted to hear and as mentioned before, if there is a possibility of a good grand slam being available — and remember that West has at no stage limited his hand — the 5♠ cue bid just leaves room for partner to bid the grand slam if this is the information that he is seeking. The jump to 7♣ becomes completely obvious when you think about it. On any lead one can draw trumps and as opener is known to have only three cards in spades and diamonds, after drawing the trumps then a loser from the West hand can be discarded on the three winning hearts.

I am the first to admit that one can always produce hands to suit certain circumstances. We can all produce hands to demonstrate the efficiency of our methods. I am much more interested in more overall efficiency of method and I think that 'efficiency' is the key word to all top class bidding. The word that I have used a lot is 'rhythm', and I have said before, really top class bidders seem to be having a relaxed conversation with each other, and that conversation is communicative because their vocabulary is so wide that many shades of meaning can be introduced into the conversation.

I have done no more than to suggest to natural bidders a philosophy of thinking, a way of thinking that has been proved to be successful at the highest possible levels over many years. I have only, however, introduced you to a suggested basic approach, the surface has hardly been scratched. But if aspiring partnerships adopt a method that is based on a solid foundation, and then explore for themselves, they will find a multitude of ways to give their vocabulary greater and greater definition.

One of the most vital things about introducing new ideas into a system is that whenever you take a bid and give it a new conventional or partnership meaning, it loses its use in any other sense. One must therefore be certain to weigh the benifits to be gained against the loss of a natural bid. Even more important is that such a bid must become completely lodged in one's memory so that it never leads to disaster. It is pointless having just some general agreement that one will adopt some particular convention or conventional idea if the convention only occurs rarely, and one disaster will need a lot of triumphs to redress the balance. So my strongest pleas to all the pairs that wish to reach the top in the field of bidding, is that they should practice their bidding to make absolutely sure that their conversation is fluent and to ensure that at the table they are never left in a situation of wondering what on earth a bid means. If a partnership has done the job properly they will find that with a little thought they will always be able to work out logically exactly what partner's bid means.

Index